Develop Your
Marketing Skills

THE SUNDAY TIMES

CREATING SUCCESS

Develop Your
Marketing Skills

Ruth Gosnay and Neil Richardson

KOGAN
PAGE

London and Philadelphia

First published in Great Britain and the United States in 2008 by Kogan Page Limited

120 Pentonville Road
London N1 9JN
United Kingdom
www.koganpage.com

525 South 4th Street, #241
Philadelphia PA 19147
USA

© Ruth Gosnay and Neil Richardson, 2008

The right of Ruth Gosnay and Neil Richardson to be identified as the authors of this work has been asserted by them in accordance with the Copyright, Designs and Patents Act 1988.

ISBN 978 0 7494 5395 4

British Library Cataloguing-in-Publication Data

A CIP record for this book is available from the British Library.

Library of Congress Cataloging-in-Publication Data

Gosnay, Ruth.
  Develop your marketing skills / Ruth Gosnay and Neil Richardson.
    p. cm.
  ISBN 978-0-7494-5395-4
  1. Marketing. 2. Marketing--Management. 3. Strategic planning. I. Richardson, Neil. II. Title.
    HF5415.G618 2008
    658.8--dc22
                                                    2008019367

Typeset by Jean Cussons Typesetting, Diss, Norfolk
Printed and bound in India by Replika Press Pvt Ltd

338006

Contents

Introduction

First may we take this opportunity to thank you for buying this book. Having bought it you are now one of our customers, which means a lot to us. As you progress through the chapters you'll see the theme of customers being the single most important stakeholder in a marketer's professional life.

If you're not specifically a marketer you may wonder whether marketing really matters. Suffice to say that substantial research (in the United States) found that the largest single cause of corporate failure was organisations not marketing themselves effectively. This was followed by poor financial control and plain 'bad' management.

As senior lecturers at Leeds Business School we have considerable experience of teaching across the whole range of ages, industrial experiences, organisational types and markets. In teaching Chartered Institute of Marketing (CIM) students we're often asked a diverse range of questions. We've encapsulated these questions in this text and offered honest, sometimes critical answers. The CIM students are professionals studying in their spare time and they are truly representative of the whole spectrum of organisations involved in marketing.

This book is aimed at practitioners who don't have the time to trawl through 1,200-page tomes. That said, our approach of using examples to apply marketing theories will offer insights into the theories missing from many key marketing texts. We're confident that you'll find new information that will enable you to develop your knowledge, skills and, we hope, attitude. These are the key building blocks for developing managers.

Throughout the text we've suggested activities based on reality designed to encourage you to re-evaluate your surroundings. Questions are posed after most chapters, with answers in Chapter 12. Despite having decades of private sector experience between us, we're academics after all!

So once again, thanks for the order, enjoy the book.

Marketing: separating fact from fiction

Most people, when asked what marketing is all about, usually give the following responses:

Advertising! Sales! Products! Free gifts!
Research!

This isn't unusual. These words often describe what most people think marketing represents, whether they're students or indeed fellow professionals who work in industry.

The descriptive words above certainly form part of the jigsaw puzzle of what the world of marketing constitutes, but marketing itself is so much more. This is one of the first myths of marketing that needs dispelling. Marketing is not just about advertising and promotional work. People perceive it as such because promotional work, whether it be advertising, PR or sales promotional activity, is often the most visible part of a marketing team's effort to the outside world.

The second myth that needs dispelling, one most people, even those who work in business often believe, is that marketing is just a function of business that merely churns out products, free gifts and advertising matter from employees who work in the marketing department. However, marketing is much deeper and significantly more profound than this.

If marketing is used and truly understood and implemented correctly in a business, it becomes a philosophy, a way of doing business – a whole approach, which should and must permeate throughout an entire organisation. Hence, marketing is everybody's responsibility, not just the specialist marketers who work in the marketing department.

Why is it everybody's responsibility?

Well, think about it logically. How many times have you phoned an organisation and been cut off, or not spoken to in a professional manner, or not been given the answers you deserve? How many times have you visited organisations as a customer and your feet stick to the floors because they haven't been cleaned properly, or you meet staff who haven't been trained to deal with questions and queries?

The reason marketing is everybody's responsibility is quite simple, yet incredibly important – it is because we all play a part in creating the 'customer experience'.

So – what actually is it?

If one word had to be chosen to encapsulate the central focus of marketing it would be 'customer'. Marketing is about understanding who your customers are, being able to anticipate what they require now and in the future and, ultimately, satisfying their every need. All the work your organisation undertakes (not just the marketing department) should therefore be created and implemented to serve the customer.

The definition put forward by the Chartered Institute of Marketing (see www.cim.co.uk) is a sound one; it describes marketing as 'the management process responsible for identifying, anticipating and satisfying customer requirements profitably'. This definition is useful in understanding the key facets of what marketing is truly all about as it is direct, concise and almost every word means something that is critical to understanding exactly what the marketing philosophy entails.

The first three words of this definition are particularly important in understanding marketing. First, marketing is now seen as being of senior management importance, being strategic as well as tactical and operational. For it to be truly embedded into the culture and heart of an organisation, it needs commitment from top management, and in many organisations today a marketing director will be on the board to lead the organisation forwards with a marketing-based awareness.

Secondly, marketing is a process. There is no clinical start and end. It isn't linear. It's continual – a process – it never stops or ends. As the world changes, so do our customers, hence our businesses adapt and evolve to move with the times.

Before we can satisfy the customer we must truly understand who they are as well as we possibly can – we must identify them. Marketing isn't just about the here and now either. It is also about the future. Marketers must 'anticipate' customer wants and needs. Why? Again, think about it logically. It may take your organisation years to develop a new product (or service) and launch it into the market. Therefore, you must think into the future in terms of the customers' desires and needs and not just their current requirements.

If your organisation can identify and anticipate customer requirements, you can move to try and satisfy them. But, once again, there is an added complication. Most organisations have limited resources: financial, staff, equipment, etc. Therefore, an organisation must seek to satisfy its customers efficiently (with as little wastage as possible) and profitably. However, now more than ever, business activities should also be undertaken and managed in an ethical and socially responsible manner.

The marketing concept

Your organisation's most important 'asset' is your customers. Irrespective of whether your company is a product- or service-based organisation or indeed a charity, you must place the customer at the heart of all the decision making and planning (not just the marketing) decisions. Where customer needs drive all the business decisions a marketing philosophy has been truly adopted and implemented. This is generally known as the 'marketing concept'.

This can only be achieved by entering into regular, honest dialogue with your customers. Every time you receive customer feedback your organisation grows stronger, as shown in Figure 1.1.

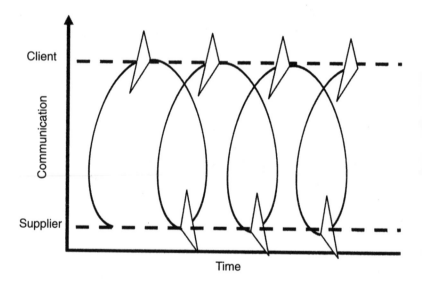

Figure 1.1 *Healthy dialogue with clients benefits all parties*

An organisation that adopts the marketing concept into its business practices is therefore said to be 'marketing-oriented'.

Are all organisations marketing-oriented?

Unfortunately not! There are a number of different business orientations that organisations tend to follow. Have a look at them below.

Production orientation

This is where the managers are focused not upon the customer but upon production techniques, reduced costs and efficiency issues. Typically it involves high volume, low margin business with low R&D or innovation. To use an analogy, if China were a company, it would be production-oriented. Is this approach to running a business incorrect? Not necessarily, but it is very inward-looking. What if the market, competition and customers change? How will an organisation following this inward-looking approach know to change accordingly? In reality, it probably wouldn't, which is a major disadvantage of this approach if adopted in today's highly competitive, fast-paced marketplace.

Product orientation

This is where an organisation focuses upon the product it produces: the features, quality, cost and brand, etc – *not* the customer. Typically these companies look to augment existing products or improve on competitors' products. Again, is this a suitable approach and philosophy for running a business? Well, yes, for some.

The Apple iPod is a simply brilliant concept but many of its components have existed for decades (displays, hard disks, etc) and it wasn't the first MP3 player to market. The Virgin organisation has had huge success at taking on major players in new markets and doing it in its own 'Virgin way'. That said, Virgin and Apple are exceptions to the rule and most product-oriented organisations adopt an inward focus at their own peril! Again, it has to be acknowledged that even with an inward-looking approach to running a business, the product may be successful initially, but what if newer, more innovative and competitive products appear in the market? What if the initial customer response to the new product is negative? Will product-oriented businesses be best positioned to respond? Arguably not.

Sales orientation

This approach is where an organisation introduces sales techniques to sell its products; basically it sells whatever it produces. This approach became popular in the 1950s, when customers were starting to be given a choice of products and services – in other words, when competition started to really appear in the marketplace. Hard-sell techniques were often used in this approach to help persuade the customer to buy one particular product or service rather than that of the competition. A useful approach? Yes it certainly can be but again, organisations must be cautious if they use this sole approach today.

A more enlightened example of a sales-oriented company is Dell. Anyone who takes a subscription, say, to *The Times* can't help but notice Dell's massive investment in advertising. Hundreds of days every year there are half- and full-page ads, not to mention ads on TV, radio and other media. A straw poll of our classes over the last few years has never failed to produce a cluster of students who have bought Dell machines. Dell didn't invent the PC, it's probably not the cheapest unit in the market but you have to go a long way to find a company that advertises its PCs more effectively than Dell.

These orientations are summarised in Table 1.1.

The benefits of being marketing-oriented

By embracing the marketing concept and placing the customer at the heart of all planning and decision making you should

Table 1.1 *Attributes of different orientations*

Orientation	Nature	Motivation to change	Marketing activities	Marketing oriented
Production	Stack 'em high sell 'em cheap – high volume, low margin, risk, R & D and innovation	*Internal* Take share by cost leadership	*Yes* Often target late majority and laggards (see Chapter 5)	No
Product	Add to existing ideas. Some tailoring of product offer. Medium volume, occasionally high margins	*Internal* Look to improve on internal or external rivals	*Yes* Target early adopters and niche markets	No
Sales	'We sell what we produce.' Not necessarily the first nor the best. Can take large market share	*Internal* Look to take share from competitors by having higher awareness. Single transactions	*Yes* Heavy reliance on promotion – some use of mass media, others through sales teams. Strong branding	No
Marketing	'We sell what our customers want'. Often end up market leaders. Seek to innovate with products and services	*External* Seek to identify customer needs that aren't satisfied by rivals and provide solutions. Look to develop relationships	*Yes* Heavy reliance on market research. Promote loyalty schemes. Seek to sell benefits and add value for customers	Yes

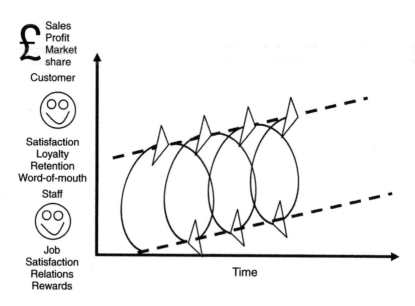

Figure 1.2 *Benefits of adopting a marketing orientation*

attain a number of key advantages, as shown in Figure 1.2 and listed below:

- increase in market share;
- increase in turnover;
- increase in profitability;
- increase in customer satisfaction;
- increase in customer loyalty;
- increase in the number of new users;
- creating a competitive advantage.

Put quite simply, if you continually give customers what they want, the chances are that they will come back, time and time again to purchase your product or services, therefore enhancing sales, turnover and profitability as well as gaining customer satisfaction and loyalty. Satisfied customers tend to not only return to purchase for themselves once again, they also tend to tell their friends, families and colleagues. Conversely, if they have a poor experience, they tend to tell even more people about it!

Why does my company need to be marketing-oriented?

Consider the world we live in today. For many organisations, the marketplace is a difficult, dynamic, dangerous and highly competitive place to be. To be more successful, your organisation must be externally focused, not just internally focused upon production techniques, products and sales issues. A much wider view is needed. You certainly need excellent production techniques, products and sales initiatives but an awareness of the customer and other factors at play in the wider environment is paramount. Wherever and whenever you see changes in the market or environment, you must change and adapt, otherwise you risk being left behind and could suffer quite serious repercussions.

Many organisations develop a tunnel-like vision to their business activities. This condition is often referred to as 'marketing myopia' – a short-sightedness that can often result in the loss of customers and eventually loss of the business. Nowadays many academics and practitioners subscribe to the view that the business environment is changing at such a rate that we're all working in permanent turbulence and our planned strategies have little chance of reaching their intended goals without deflection.

It is easy to get ensnared into analysing and crunching sales and market share figures, focusing upon staffing issues, buying in new capital equipment and other such internal matters. However, one of the central issues to developing a marketing philosophy and culture throughout an organisation is to place just as much emphasis on external matters.

Why focus upon the customer and not concentrate on core organisational strengths?

Simply put, it is the customer that purchases products and services from an organisation in exchange for money. This exchange process brings the organisation and the customer together. If customers have a positive experience with the product or service, or with the overall experience, they will tell their family, friends and colleagues, and if they have a bad experience the chances are that they will tell even more people about it. This applies now more than ever with the advent of the internet. Web 2.0 has seen an explosion in the number of user websites (see www.imdb.com), blogs and social network sites such as Facebook. In 2007 Cadbury re-launched its Wispa bar as a result of a campaign on Facebook for bringing it back. Good for Cadbury for monitoring the external environment. As electronic exchanges can bring the two parties together, a relationship is formed and many marketers today try to capitalise upon that initial relationship by finding out as much as they can about the customers and their needs.

Customers are also constantly changing and technology is enabling quicker, easier decision making – for instance by using cost-comparison websites such as Kelkoo or Pricecompare. com. As customers change, their desires, needs and wants also change and if an organisation doesn't change and adapt with them, the chances are that they will dissatisfy the customer and start to lose their customers to the competition.

Another myth that also requires dispelling is that the whole marketing effort is only used by large organisations with huge budgets. On the contrary, it can be argued that the marketing philosophy is even more important for a small business to engage in than it is for a global or multinational player. Small businesses don't have the low cost base or the huge pool of investment funds that are available to a large business. However, they often have an advantage in their ability to move much closer to customers, to form a strong alliance with them and make them feel incredibly important. They can also move flexibly and quickly with changing customer needs and market dynamics. Therefore the marketing philosophy can be embraced and implemented in any size or type of organisation. Indeed it's worth reiterating that irrespective of your organisational size or type, it is imperative that you monitor the external forces that can impact on the customer.

What are these external factors?

Basically, as the world constantly evolves and changes, so customers change what they require. Organisations that don't adapt and change with the times are often those that eventually have to fight for their very survival. Marketing is about not only satisfying customers but delighting them. It's about adding value, quality and innovation to their experiences but in an ethical and socially responsible manner.

Just think about what happened to Marks & Spencer in the 1990s. This powerful giant took its eye off its core customers whose needs were changing; and new competition had entered the high street and the wider external environment. As a consequence, it suffered tremendous losses. Fortunately, it was able to make massive changes that permeated to the core of its management culture and fed through to a process of recovery, where the focus of its philosophy changed to become one of identifying, anticipating and delighting the customer.

Others such as the retailer C&A weren't so lucky and lost their fight for survival. You no longer see this store on the UK high street. Professor Malcolm McDonald argues (in his excellent *Marketing Planning* book from Kogan Page) that marketing in the UK has gone backwards in the last 10 years. This may be attributed to excessive internal organisational focus on 'systems' rather than external factors such as customers and competitors. These issues will be looked at in more depth in Chapter 2.

Key points

- Remember that the customer should be at the heart of all business and marketing decisions and activities.
- An organisation should be both internally and externally focused to truly understand and react to changing customer needs and trends.
- Researching who your customers are and what they want is a start to developing a relationship with them.

- Providing your customers with what they want by anticipating their needs and satisfying them will entice them to come back time and time again.
- As time moves on, customer needs change and your marketing-related activities need to change with them.

Activities

Think about your behaviour as a consumer. How have your needs changed as you've grown older? Can you think of any organisations that satisfy your needs really well, which encourages you to go back time and time again? Likewise, can you think of any organisations that have disappointed you? If you have been disappointed, how would you advise them to improve?

Questions (answers in Chapter 12)

1. Explain the marketing concept.
2. What are the key benefits that an organisation can attain by becoming marketing-oriented?
3. Many organisations that embrace a product orientation can initially achieve huge success. What problems could such organisations face in the future?
4. Why is marketing the responsibility of everybody throughout an organisation?
5. What steps can you take to build a marketing philosophy into your organisation's culture?
6. Consider your own organisation. Does it currently embrace a production, sales or market orientation?

The marketing environment

By now you should have a better understanding about what marketing represents and why your organisation needs to continually satisfy customers.

Just take a minute to think about how the world has changed over the last 30 years. Technology has accelerated the rate of change in ways that have affected our lives beyond recognition. Therefore, every organisation has to continually monitor the factors that are operating outside the organisation as well as inside it, to ensure it changes with the times. These factors are known collectively in marketing terms as the 'marketing environment'.

The marketing environment consists of, 1) those factors that are external and beyond the control of the organisation – they are known collectively as the 'macro environment' or the 'situational environment' – *and*, 2) those factors that are more specific to particular industries or sectors and where an organisation, to a degree, has a certain amount of control over them; this is often referred to as the 'micro environment' (see Figure 2.1). Let's take a look at the macro environment first.

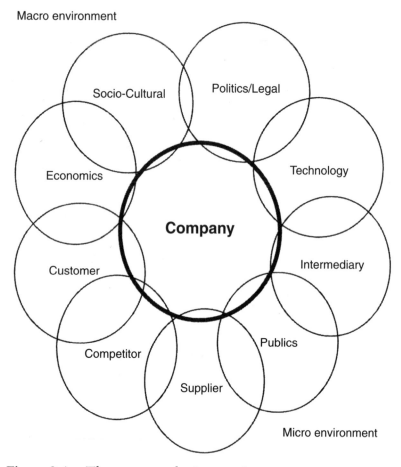

Figure 2.1 *The macro and micro environments*

The macro environment

The macro environment is perhaps the most feared by businesses as it consists of a set of uncontrollable factors that are external to the organisation.

If they are uncontrollable, why does an organisation need to know about them?

Good question. Even though the organisation cannot control what happens in the external environment, the factors within it can have a massive impact upon a business. Therefore, there is a key need to monitor these factors closely and, if possible, to take advantage of the opportunities that arise and to steer clear of the underlying threats.

Although there are potential threats that can adversely affect your business if not addressed appropriately, the macro environment can also be viewed as highly positive, because it also provides many substantial opportunities for your business to exploit, giving it the ability to grow and prosper.

The factors in the macro environment

The acronym 'PEST' is often used to describe the key factors that make up the macro environment. PEST stands for the following factors:

Political
Economical
Social/Cultural and
Technological

Other acronyms are derived from PEST such as:

PESTLE where the Legal and Environmental elements are featured.
STEEPLE where Ethical considerations are monitored.
EPISTLE where Information is deemed worthy of consideration.
STEEL PIE is little known but covers all of the factors.

Ultimately you need to decide which tool best suits your organisation. For example, a charity will probably use STEEPLE due

to the ethical angle, whilst new technology companies would
see information as key and so use EPISTLE. Let's have a look at
the key PEST factors in more detail.

Political factors

The government of any country has the ability to affect organisations and consumers. It can introduce new legislation that
can affect organisations and customers alike.

Example: New legislation has recently been passed to liber-
alise gaming laws allowing casinos, bingo halls and sport
betting under one roof. This could attract wealthier people to
UK tourist destinations and a number of businesses could see
this as a huge opportunity.

Economic factors

Within the economy, factors such as unemployment rates,
interest rates, taxation and exchange rates can all affect your
business and consumers.

Example: If interest rates are high, consumers are left with
less disposable income for products and services. The UK prop-
erty market was recently valued at £4 trillion of which a third is
linked to debt/lending. Hence if interest rates are lowered, it
arguably has a greater impact than, say, tax cuts.

Social/cultural factors

Socially, factors such as age, sex, income and occupation affect
what customers demand. Culturally, factors such as religion,
language, values and beliefs can also affect what customers
demand and require.

Example 1: As the role of women in society has changed over
the years, many organisations are targeting women with
specific products and services, eg the car industry.

Example 2: Language is a key issue for marketers.
Unfortunately, organisations that have tried to launch products
overseas have often forgotten about the language differences.
An interesting insight can be gained by asking colleagues what
they consider to be the language of business. Let them offer the

usual suspects (English, French, Spanish, Mandarin, etc) before explaining that, simply put, the language of business is the language of the customer.

Technology

The arrival of the internet and related information communication technologies (ICT) has changed the way we run our lives in relatively recent years.

Example: EasyJet uses the internet as its prime means of communicating with its customers, allowing them to search for flights and book online. Where does this leave the future of travel agents?

Why be concerned with the macro environment if it's uncontrollable?

While the macro environment is uncontrollable, its impact can have a dramatic impact on your organisation. You therefore need to continually monitor and scan the external environment looking for any particular trends, issues or factors that may eventually affect you. If you do this, you can take advantage of any key opportunities that may arise. EasyJet has taken full advantage of the introduction and widespread use of the internet to create and develop a successful brand and product. By keeping an eye on the external environment, organisations may also be able to spot any key threats to their business and try to steer clear of them. If they don't, it could lead them into serious danger, which they may find difficult to recover from.

Always ensure that you undertake current analysis on your external environment. To help you identify the key factors, use the PEST framework.

Now, let's take a look at the micro environment in more detail.

The micro environment

As stated earlier, this consists of factors that are close to the organisation and may affect its ability to serve its customers. These factors usually consist of:

■ suppliers;
■ distributors/intermediaries;
■ competitors;
■ customers;
■ publics (employees, management, shareholders, etc).

Suppliers

Very few organisations can create a product or service on their own. We often need suppliers to help us. They are usually a vital component of any organisation and some would state are in fact a 'partner' in our obligations to satisfy customers.

Example 1: Think about a pair of Levi's jeans. A supplier has provided Levi's with the raw materials to produce the denim, the rivets, the thread needed, etc so it can create the jeans. If a supplier stopped providing Levi's with any of these components or the materials to create the denim themselves, what would Levi's do?

Example 2: A car is deemed to be British if 60 per cent (some say 70 per cent) of its components are sourced locally. In other words 30 to 40 per cent of a 'British' car is sourced globally.

Distributors

Many organisations use intermediaries such as retailers to get their product to the customer.

Example: Tefal uses retailers such as Argos, Currys and Comet to place its products in the marketplace so that it is convenient for the end-user to purchase it. What would happen if Tefal lost its contract with these retailers? It may have a great product but if it can't get it to market then that's quite a problem.

Competitors

Our competitors can affect what we produce, how we price our produce, where we sell, etc. Most organisations need to be competitive. If they are not, customers will purchase their competitors' products.

Example 1: The UK grocery retail sector is extremely competitive. Over the next few weeks just keep an eye on how much press coverage organisations such as Asda, Tesco and Morrisons gain, the deals they launch, the cut prices they highlight and the ads they run on TV. They are competing heavily against each other and are often vying for customers.

Example 2: When Renault heavily promoted its NCAP safety ratings, all car manufacturers selling into the EU responded in kind.

Example 3: The Nintendo Wii has had, arguably, the most successful games console launch ever. It offers a different functionality to other more expensive consoles and you can be sure that Sony and Microsoft will respond.

Customers

We need to listen to our customers and monitor their preferences, habits and attitudes. As they change, an organisation also needs to change to be able to continue providing the products and services the customer demands. If an organisation ceases to satisfy a customer, quite simply the customer will go elsewhere.

Example 1: One of the key reasons Marks and Spencer fell from grace in the 1990s was that it did not recognise that the needs and wants of its core target market had changed.

Publics

These are individuals or groups who have a vested interest in the activities of an organisation. It could be the local community, pressure groups, the media, even the employees.

Example 1: Due to past controversial advertising, Benetton was the subject of active lobbying by concerned parties. This lobbying and demonstrations affected its level of sales and plans to open further stores, particularly across the United States.

Example 2: The rebranding of French Connection to FCUK led to a 400 per cent increase in UK turnover. However, it had nothing like the same success in the United States where consumers are deemed to be somewhat more reserved in terms of sexual innuendo.

Employees

(A key component of publics, hence worthy of closer consideration.) We must always remember the people who work for and with us. Without their effort, skill and knowledge we quite simply would not have an organisation. We have just as much responsibility to respect and value our colleagues and form trustworthy relationships with them as we do with our suppliers and distributors. Hundreds of studies have shown the benefits to be gained from treating staff well. Employees are consistently one of the best sources of new ideas and information. This is unfortunately an aspect that many managers fail to recognise to the extent that they should.

Do marketers really have control over the micro environment?

They certainly have influence! Your organisation has relationships with these groups. Therefore, strengthening these relationships and investing in them and listening to each other helps to create a more settled environment.

Again, the issue of relationships is rearing its head. A key skill of effective marketers is to identify the key groups with whom they need to communicate and develop meaningful relationships over the long term.

Monitoring the micro/macro environments

To keep up to date with all the changes occurring within and around your organisation, a monitoring system needs to be employed.

For monitoring factors in your macro environment, simple things such as keeping up to date with current affairs by reading newspapers, or logging onto the BBC news website on a daily basis are a start, but we can become more sophisticated. Government statistics are published regularly, showing trends in population, age, immigration and migration, death rates or divorce rates. This is key social information that you may find useful to monitor. The government and local authorities also publish national and local economic information on employment status, economic growth, average income, occupation, etc that you may find useful.

With regard to monitoring factors in your micro environment, visiting trade shows and collecting competitor information from the stands and reading articles in the trade press can help you keep up to date with competitors. Regular contact and feedback with sales teams can help to create two-way communication with customers, whether they are end-user customers or business-to-business customers. Regular and accurate communication and the exchange of information are essential in the development of a trusting relationship.

What you need to be is creative, yet practical, to create simple yet effective monitoring systems that will help you keep an eye on the dynamic marketing environment. Work with your local business school. At Leeds Business School we have a long tradition of supporting local, national and international businesses.

What you also need to understand is that the marketing environment can be very different in the various markets you serve. A key weakness of many organisations is that they try to emulate success in one market with the same magical formula in another. Caution is needed. For example, the marketing environment in your domestic market may be quite different in an international market where the political climate, the economy and the social environment may be constructed very differently. Therefore you need to undertake a separate analysis for each market you serve.

The marketing environment is extremely powerful. As mentioned previously, it can create many potential opportunities for an organisation; however, it can also be the cause of many problems and underlying threats to the business. If you ignore the marketing environment – you do so at your own peril!

Key points

■ The marketing environment basically consists of two parts: the macro and the micro environment.

■ The macro environment is uncontrollable and consists of external factors such as political, economic, social/cultural and technological issues.

■ Although the macro environment is uncontrollable, marketers must develop systems to continually monitor and scan the external environment to be able to take advantage of any opportunities the changing environment presents and minimise the threats that occur.

■ The micro environment has an element of control and consists of an organisation's customers, suppliers, intermediaries, competitors and publics.

■ The development of relationships, particularly with people in the micro environment, is central to effective marketing.

Activities

Taking British Airways (BA) as an example, apply the PEST framework to the organisation. What are the political and legal issues currently affecting BA? Are there any current or potentially new economic issues or changes it needs to be aware of? What about any cultural or social issues? Are changes in technology going to affect this organisation? How?

By doing this exercise it is easy to see just how complex the marketing environment can be and how numerous the issues are. Once you've had a practice, try to apply the PEST framework to your own organisation.

Questions

1. What are the factors in the macro environment?
2. Identify the frameworks you can choose from to use in a macro environmental analysis.
3. Identify the parties that create your micro environment.
4. Why is the micro environment partly controllable?

Customers in all their glory

Why do marketers need to understand how consumers behave?

Have you ever stopped and considered why you are shopping in the manner that you are? Why you are shopping in a particular location? Or shop? Have a look at the products and brands in your shopping trolley the next time you go food shopping. Are you purchasing own-label brands? Premium brands? Why? What causes you to reach out and select a particular product? Routine? Experience? Impulse? Apathy?

If we understand how and why consumers behave in a certain way, we can provide them with information and resources to facilitate their decision making. It's particularly useful to know how customers behave when they are buying our products or services and what influences these processes.

Before we have a look at customers' buying behaviour we need to be clear on who we mean when we refer to a customer. Generally speaking there are two markets: 'business-to-consumer' (B2C) and 'business-to-business' (B2B).

The consumer market

This is the market where consumers (end-users) buy the product or service for their own personal consumption.

Example: If you go shopping on Saturday afternoon and go into GAP to buy a new pair of jeans to go home and wear that evening, you are acting as a consumer and GAP is operating in the consumer market.

The business-to-business market (B2B)

Also referred to as the 'industrial market', the customer for some organisations is often another organisation.

Example: Dyson sells its vacuum cleaners through retailers such as Argos, Comet and Currys. These retailers are Dyson's customers. Dyson is operating initially in the B2B market whereas Comet *et al* are in the B2C market.

Now we've got that issue settled, let's move on and look at how customers behave when they buy our products and/or services.

How do consumers buy a product or service?

For the purposes of this section there is no difference between buying products and buying services. (The differences are discussed later, in Chapter 9.) Consumers generally move through a psychological process when purchasing products. This is often referred to as the 'consumer buying process' or the 'decision-making process' and it contains a number of simple steps, shown in Figure 3.1. Let's take each step and have a look in closer detail.

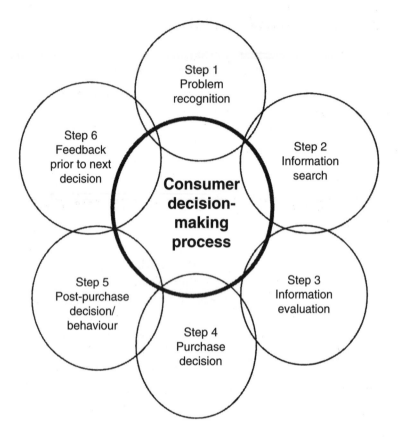

Figure 3.1 *Consumer decision-making process*

Consumer buying process

1. Problem recognition

Most consumers start the buying process when they realise there's a problem, for example their washing machine's broken or they may want some new clothes to go out in on Saturday night, their car may be constantly letting them down, and so on.

2. Information search
After a problem has been recognised the consumer then searches for information to try and rectify the problem. This information search could involve looking at websites on the internet, reading magazines, visiting retail outlets, or asking friends or family for advice.

3. Information evaluation
The customer may see two or three different options that suit his or her needs and then has to sit down and evaluate what he or she can get out of each deal.

4. Purchasing decision
Once they've weighed up the pros and cons, customers then make their final decision and purchase their chosen item.

5 and 6. Post-purchase decision and feedback
Once they have worn their new item of clothing, they may find that it falls to pieces the first time they wash it and decide never to buy that brand again! Their car may still be going strong and be reliable several years later. This could lead to them purchasing the same product/brand again.

There are various means to record customer feedback, such as the JD Power survey, which gathers consumer opinions on three-year-old cars and covers a range of issues such as reliability, economy and service quality. New digital technologies have changed the way consumers can exert post-purchase influence, for instance posting their views on blogs, websites and social networks.

Hopefully there is also a learning process as consumers move through this sequence. What is learnt should be fed back into the process as it's revisited.

Do all consumers move through this process?

Yes they do! No matter what products are purchased, consumers always move through this process. However, they often do so at different speeds depending on what items are being bought.

When buying a brand new car it can take months to move through this process as consumers spend a lot of time searching for information. The decision they make has risks, socially and financially. Even with the assistance of price comparison and review websites, most people need to test drive cars prior to buying. However, when the same person runs out of bread, he or she moves through this process in minutes if not seconds. This is primarily due to there being little risk financially or personally and because this is considered to be a habitual purchase. Most consumers have bought such items regularly – they simply don't have to think about it a great deal.

Are there factors that affect what and how consumers buy?

Absolutely! Age, sex, income, education, personality, attitudes, motivation and perception are a few.

Age
Think about how your choices of what to buy have changed as you have grown older.

Income
Unfortunately, when we intend buying large items we can't always buy what we want (the S Type Jaguar is still on hold). Instead we choose goods more in line with our income.

Attitude/perception
We often stipulate features for emotional reasons. Some people won't buy brown cars. Why? Completely irrational! But the consumer may have long-standing negativity, which we need to identify before we can complete the selling process.

Social factors – culture, reference groups, social class
There are many products and services that are particularly sensitive to cultural differences, such as foodstuffs. The role of

the family has deep meaning and belief for many cultures. What this means from a marketing perspective is that many purchase decisions often involve more than one member of the family. We may have a friend who had nothing but problems with a certain car. Again, we're influenced by family and friends (sometimes unduly), particularly when buying high-tech items where the salespeople know considerably more than our peers.

Why do marketers need to understand this process?

By understanding that consumers go through the consumer buying process, marketers can develop additional marketing-related activities to help consumers to make the right decision. An effective marketer would understand, for example, that the purchase of a new car is a serious decision that is risky financially, socially and personally. So, to help reduce the amount (or at least the perception) of risk with decisions and to make consumers feel more informed and comfortable, marketers should provide a wide variety of additional materials and activities to relay the benefits on offer. It's about the benefits that solve customer problems, not simply listing features.

When they buy a loaf of bread, consumers don't have magazines or colourful brochures available on the shelf to help with the decision-making process. Why? Because this is a completely different type of product (which will be discussed in more detail later) with a very different level of risk associated with its purchase. Marketers know that most people do not spend more than a few minutes searching for information and evaluating the alternatives before making their purchase decision for a loaf of bread. By understanding how consumers purchase products and services, we can create the correct materials, environments and additional activities to support them. Indeed we can start to categorise the different types of decisions or problems that consumers need to solve.

Routine problem solving

This type of problem can usually be solved relatively quickly with little expense and risk involved for the customer. Items such as bread, vegetables and fruit fall into this category as they tend to be habitual purchases. There is often little thought that goes into purchasing them, so the customer will go through the stages of the above process quickly and little marketing-related support activities are required.

Limited problem solving

This type of problem tends not to be as quick to solve as the previous category. Products such as washing machines and DVD players may fall into this group. The customer will spend longer moving through the decision-making stages as the purchases involve more risks, mainly financial, but customers have less experience of purchasing these products as the previous category. By nature, the products purchased here also tend to represent a longer commitment for customers: they will buy a new washing machine to last them several years.

Extended problem solving

This situation tends to involve the purchase of products and services that require a great deal of consideration beforehand. The customer will take some time moving through the decision-making process, primarily because the products/services are high risk for them. This could be financial risk, social risk (what will people think of me if I buy this product/brand?), performance risk or indeed ego risk (will this product/brand make me feel good?). If you were buying a car, which you regard as expensive, you naturally will want to take your time making the right decision for you. The same applies to buying a house or a wedding dress. These types of purchase also tend to feature long-term commitment and the products will be around for some time.

Organisational buying behaviour

Organisations that operate in the B2B market also go through a buying process but it differs to the consumer model; see Figure 3.2. This is because of a number of differences in the factors relating to buyer behaviour. For example, compared to the consumer market, the B2B market tends to have fewer buyers.

The buyers in the B2B market tend to be highly trained in the art of buying and negotiating. With the exception of when we are on our annual holiday abroad and try our hand at haggling, consumers generally don't go in for negotiation.

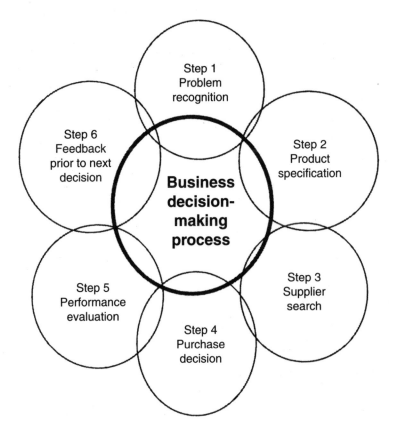

Figure 3.2   *Business decision-making process*

Buyers in the B2B market tend to buy in huge quantities – consumers don't. Asda buys a huge volume of televisions to sell in its stores, while consumers tend to buy one or two for their own home.

So how does this process work?

Again, it's pretty simple:

1. Problem recognition: A company that manufactures televisions has run out of screens – it therefore has a problem.
2. Product specification: The buyer then, often with technical help, identifies exactly what type of screens it needs and what quantity.
3. Supplier search: As it knows exactly what type of screen it requires, the company then searches for a supplier that can provide it with the quality and quantity of screens it needs, at the right price.
4. Purchase decision: Once it has found a suitable supplier it then places the order through its formal ordering procedures.
5 and 6. Performance evaluation and feedback: How did the screens perform? Have there been any complaints from manufacturing staff? Or the end consumer?

So are there other influences on business buyers?

Yes, there are quite a few, which we discuss below.

Environmental factors
These include economic uncertainty, legislation, basically all of the PEST factors mentioned in Chapter 2.

Organisational factors
The organisation's objectives, policies, procedures and systems need to be taken into account. There are also economic (small 'e') factors such as price, lead-time, after-sales support, warranty, etc.

Non-economic or interpersonal factors

Despite what some salespeople may think, buyers are human! Factors such as age, sex, expertise, relationships, prestige, reputation, career stage, ambition, attitude to risk, etc can all affect the buying process.

Whether you work and operate in the consumer or B2B market (or both), consider the length of the buying process for your customers and the degree of risk involved for them. Are they in a routine, limited or extensive problem-solving situation? Identify the key influential factors affecting their decision making. If you can determine these factors, you are starting to establish a deeper understanding of how your customers behave and what influences them. This is important information and feeds into the more practical aspects of the marketing arena that are needed to support their decision making; we will look at these shortly.

Key points

- The consumer buying process consists of five basic steps: problem recognition, information search, information evaluation, purchase decision, and post-purchase decision and feedback.
- Consumers are influenced in their buying behaviour by social, personal and psychological factors.
- Organisations also have customers that are other businesses (B2B).
- A buyer who works in an organisation will also go through a buying process, which includes: problem recognition, product specification, supplier search, purchasing, and performance evaluation and feedback.
- Organisational buyers are also influenced by personal, organisational and environmental factors.
- A consumer tends to spend more time searching for information when purchasing products and services that are deemed risky, personally, financially or socially (or all three).

■ A marketer needs to understand how and why consumers behave in a certain way to ensure that they are supported throughout the process and have the required information to help them make confident and correct decisions.

Activities

Think of two very different items you have purchased recently. Apply the appropriate process to your purchases. What problem(s) did you have? What information did you search for? Did you consult anyone or anything to help you make your decision? How long did it take you to go through the entire process? What persuaded you to purchase that particular product or service?

Consider the product or service your organisation markets. How much risk is involved in the purchase of it and how do you currently recognise and facilitate this?

Questions

1. Identify the steps in the consumer buying process.
2. Why do some consumers take a long time moving through the consumer buying process?
3. What are the key influential factors on a consumer's buying behaviour?
4. How does purchasing differ between a consumer and a business?
5. Why do marketers need to understand how consumers/organisations behave when purchasing products and services?

Using research to make informed decisions

Before you can satisfy customers and add value to their experience, you need to understand who they are, what they require and what influences them. The way we acquire this information is through marketing research.

As a business person, consider the number of decisions you make on a daily basis. Some decisions may be fairly minor, others may be incredibly important with far-reaching consequences. Using information helps to reduce risk and create more certainty when making decisions. As we are all well aware, there is often a variety of answers or solutions when making decisions. Marketing research can help provide the information to assist you in making the most appropriate decision within a given set of circumstances or parameters.

Marketing research

The term 'marketing research' is very broad and encompasses many different 'types' of research you may be able to use, so let's consider some of them.

Market research

This is research specifically undertaken on the market, market size, volume or value of the market. This type of research is particularly useful when you have the responsibility of researching brand new markets that may be ripe for entry. Alternatively, if you change jobs, you may need to get a feel for the market and this type of research can really focus in on the key features of the specific market in which you operate.

Product research

This is research specifically on the product, product features or desirability of the product. This approach to research is often used in new product development where the core focus of your work is centred on understanding the actual product(s).

It can also be used if you start to encounter any problems with your products. For example, if the sales and market share of one of your products are falling, you could try to deduce what the actual problem is by commissioning product research. Remember all audits are inherently political as they can involve parties having to be self-critical. You can use a third party (to minimise the political fallout) such as business schools or consultants.

Distribution research

This is research into where the products ought to be sold or, more important, where the customer wants to go to purchase the goods. During the development of an entire marketing strategy, the decision as to how to distribute your product is a key one. Again, this could be a central piece of your research.

If you are new to the area of marketing research, try not to get too hung up on the different types of research. The important factor is that you truly understand what the focus of your research is to be, what information you require and what problem you are trying to solve.

Research by its very nature is quite systematic and scientific – don't let this put you off investing in it. Even if you don't collect the data yourself, you may, if you have the resources, choose to employ a marketing research agency to do it on your behalf. You still need to fully understand the process that research goes through. Why? Because you will need to control it and respond to the data once it is presented to you.

Generally speaking, all research should follow a logical approach, such as the one shown in Figure 4.1. Let's consider in more detail what is involved in conducting research.

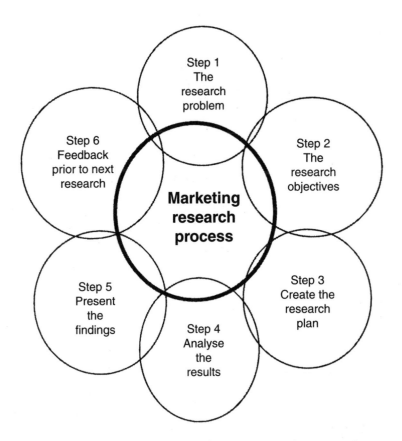

Figure 4.1 *The systematic marketing research process*

1. The research question/problem

First, it is important to define the research problem/question. Just why are you conducting this research? You will be trying to solve a particular problem or answer a particular question, for example, 'Why are the sales falling on this specific product?' or, 'What price should I charge for this new service?'

Be as specific as you can about the problem or question you wish to answer. This is an incredibly important part of the process as it serves to provide focus to the research project. Take your time considering all the issues surrounding the problem and try to define it. You can't afford to be too broad with your definition as this could create a research project that never finds the true data you want as you have cast the net too wide. Alternatively, you don't want to be too narrow with your interpretation of the problem as this could mean the net is not cast wide enough to consider all the issues that could be part of the problem – not easy.

2. Set your research objectives

Once you have identified the research problem/question, you then need to set your research objectives. Try to set SMART objectives; these are:

Specific;
Measurable;
Accurate (some say aspirational);
Realistic;
Targeted (some say timely or time-bound).

If you use SMART to help you set your research objectives, your research should become much more specific, focused and relevant to answering your research problem. Your objectives are important as they provide direction and a sense of purpose to the whole research project.

Example: To identify if brand awareness has increased by more than 3 per cent during June and July 2007, on the 'Sunshine' brand.

3. Create the research plan

The research plan contains many different factors that need consideration, for example the different types of data that you'll need, resource demands, access and so on. So assuming you now have a good understanding of what you are trying to achieve through your research and have set your objectives, let's consider the type of data required. There are two types of data: secondary and primary.

Secondary data

Generally speaking, most researchers tend to collect secondary data before primary data. This is because secondary data is data that already exists.

This data can come from internal sources such as company reports or previous market research reports. External sources such as government publications, newspapers, magazines or directories are also useful. The internet enables secondary research to a greater extent than ever before, although its scale is problematic with recent (already out of date) estimates of 65 billion pages on the web. Large research agencies, such as Mintel and Nielson, also publish research reports that you could purchase or commission. However, bought-in reports can be costly and the data is not specific to your research question, nor will it be up to date or particularly accurate. These are the key disadvantages, but 'ready-made' reports or other secondary sources may give you a starting point, or a feel, for the optimum direction.

The reason we often use and start with secondary data is because doing so is cost-effective (the data already exists), you do not need to be a skilled researcher to collect or use it, and it is relatively quick to collect. Therefore, if you work as a sole trader or in a small organisation, the use of secondary data to try to find the solution to your problem is realistically the starting point for you.

However, this will only get you so far. As this research isn't specific to helping you answer your problem/question and because it may be out of date, and therefore slightly inaccurate, the chances are that you will need to collect more up-to-date and relevant data. The data you collect for the first time, which is commissioned to be specifically focused on solving your research problem and objectives, is known as 'primary data'.

Primary data

Primary data is based on specifically answering your research problem and objectives. Therefore, it is specific, relevant, timely and, if collected and analysed properly, accurate.

There are different ways you can collect primary data. One of the factors that plays a part in deciding which technique you use is dependent upon whether you wish the research to be structured using quantitative data or qualitative data. These two terms sound intimidating but they are in fact very simple and straightforward.

Quantitative data

This refers to data based on numbers, hence 'quant/quantity'. If you are collecting secondary or primary data based upon statistics to analyse, it is quantitative data. They're usually gathered when you're seeking an answer that's representative of a larger population.

Example: When psephologist Ipsos Mori carries out research to predict UK general elections, it often uses quantitative data that aim to represent the whole voting population. It typically polls a sample of 1,500 to 2,000 prospective voters and generates results that are accurate to (+/-) 3 per cent. When it's a close run thing, 3 per cent may not be accurate enough and it would need a much larger sample or it could triangulate its findings with other surveys.

Qualitative data

This refers to 'soft' data. If you want to collect secondary or primary data that is based on people's attitudes, opinions, feelings or perceptions, then qualitative data is required. Often how we feel is a greater force than how we think. Any long-standing football fan knows that the heart rules the head, particularly for the majority of teams that rarely win trophies! Qualitative research is often used to ascertain consumers' feelings about new products or services.

It's important to understand at this early stage whether you require qualitative or quantitative data – or perhaps the use of both, which in reality is often the most suitable course of action. However, the choice is governed by your problem and your chosen research objectives.

Once you've made your choice, you then have to undertake the collection of primary data, which is quite a skilled task with a variety of methods or techniques. Here are a few of the most common ways to collect primary data.

Observation

This is when the researcher has no direct contact with the respondent; he or she is merely observing behaviour. Many psychologists use this form of research to study the difference in children's behaviour by watching them from behind a glass mirror. They may introduce a new toy to the child to see if his or her behaviour changes. From a marketing perspective, observation can be used to collect data, for example, to see the reaction of customers to the new Christmas displays in store.

Experimentation

This is where data is collected in controlled conditions. Researchers involved in scientific and medical research often use this technique, with controlled conditions in laboratories. By holding all factors constant and introducing one new factor, results can be collected as to the effect. Marketers could hold all factors relating to a new product constant and then manipulate the price at certain intervals to identify the extent to which sales are affected by increasing or lowering the price.

Questionnaires

A good questionnaire should be neither too long nor too short and should pose questions to collect the required responses to help answer the research problem/question. Generally, the type of data collected from a questionnaire is quantitative; you may not be collecting answers from the respondents that are based upon numbers but you will be able to analyse the data in a statistical manner.

Let's consider an example. One item in your questionnaire may be asking respondents which age category they fall into; see Table 4.1.

Table 4.1 *Questionnaire*

Age brackets	Under 16	16–29	30–39	40–49	50–59
No of respondents (50)	5	8	15	12	10
% (out of 50 respondents)	10%	16%	30%	24%	20%

From the data collected you can work out in percentage terms how many of your respondents were under 16, between 16 and 29, and so on.

Questionnaires provide you with the opportunity to also ask open-ended questions to collect qualitative data, for example, 'What is your opinion on banning smoking in public places?' They are also very useful if you need to collect data from a large number of people. One of the key issues to consider is that if you are dealing with a lot of people, you may not have the time, money or resources to question them all. Therefore, you will need to question a representative sample of your target audience. Always remember that the more people you question in your target audience, the greater accuracy you will gain in your results. However, as mentioned above, resource limitation may hinder you.

Focus groups

Another useful way to collect qualitative data is to use focus groups. This is where you select a number of respondents from your target audience, usually about 8–12, and ask them questions. Focus groups are very useful when you're developing new products or services as you create the opportunity to interact with a selection of your target market and perhaps show them a prototype of the product. What do they think about its design? Size? Colour? Weight? Name? How much would they pay for it? Where would they buy it? A lot of useful qualitative data can be collected.

Interviews

In-depth interviews are as useful as focus groups to collect qualitative data. The key difference between the two is that each in-depth interview is with just one respondent. Therefore, the interviewer can really probe for detailed answers, feelings, opinions, etc. However, it is very costly as it is time-consuming and on a one-to-one basis – but the results are both timely and, hopefully, accurate.

How do you choose which technique is most suitable to use?

A good question. It can be quite challenging. The trick is to really understand what it is you are trying to find out, hence the need to thoroughly understand your research problem/question and objectives, and also to appreciate which techniques are useful for collecting what type of data. You also need to consider your limitations and circumstances.

4 and 5. Analysing and presenting the findings

Once you have collected the data, whether secondary or primary, you then have to analyse it. What does it all mean? How can my company use the data? This can take time and skill, and many marketers use specialist research agencies to plan their research, collect the data and interpret and analyse it. Quantitative data is easier to analyse as it is well suited to statistical analysis, spreadsheets or simple graphs. Packages such as SPSS can facilitate complex analysis of large amounts of data. Qualitative data must still be analysed to identify themes and trends. Simply offering a few respondent quotes isn't usually enough.

Once the analysis is complete, you then need to report the findings to whoever is interested in them. This may include your manager, director, customers – not just yourself! Rest assured that good knowledge gained from well-designed research can only strengthen your company's position, so don't be surprised if others find the results and conclusions interesting as well. Put time and effort into making the report stand out. A common mistake is for researchers and marketers to make the report easy for themselves, not the reader. Have a beginning, middle and end with a logical flow from start to finish. Don't discuss things in the conclusions section that you haven't mentioned before!

Marketing research is at the heart of most marketing decisions. To remain competitive, innovative and attractive to the customer, we must constantly evolve our products, services and organisations. Marketing research is central to providing us with the data and information to help us to do this successfully. It goes without saying that the research should be conducted in an ethical fashion. If in doubt, refer to the Market Research Society's Code of Conduct.

Key points

■ Marketing research is used to give up-to-date, accurate information to help a marketer solve problems and lower the risk in important decision making.

■ Marketing research is systematic in nature and a basic process is to be followed.

■ The marketing research process includes five stages: identify the research problem, set the research objectives, develop the research plan, analyse the findings, report and present the findings.

■ Secondary data is data that already exists: it is cheap to collect, readily available and a non-skilled marketer can collect and use it. However, it is often dated, therefore inaccurate and not specific enough.

■ Primary data is data that a marketer collects for the first time. It is therefore specific, timely and accurate. However, it can be time-consuming and expensive to collect. A degree of skill is also required to collect and analyse it accurately.

■ There are a variety of techniques available to collect primary data including observation, experimentation, questionnaires, focus groups and interviews.

Activities

Look at the material in your office – past research projects, sales statistics, competitor information, pricing initiatives, etc – they could all be regarded as secondary data and could be useful to refer to in the future. Create a simple information system in your office. Ensure that you file these documents (don't throw them away). Even if you don't find them useful initially, somebody else might.

Questions

1. Why do marketers need to invest in marketing research?
2. What are the risks associated with marketing research?

3. What is secondary data? Give examples.
4. Explain what the term primary data means and give examples.
5. Why is the setting of research objectives so crucial?

Product management

Having considered what marketing represents, how research is undertaken, how consumers purchase and your organisation's marketing environment, it's now time to develop further understanding of how we actually 'do' marketing.

You've probably heard of the 'marketing mix' or, as it's more commonly known, 'the 4Ps'. The marketing mix provides the 'tools' of the trade. These four tools can be manipulated to suit the needs of the market and environment. A key issue is that the 4Ps don't stand alone, rather they interact and influence each other; see Figure 5.1.

In this chapter we're going to have a look at 'product' and the key theories and concepts we need to understand to be able to manage our products.

Product management

Many of you reading this book will have either direct or indirect responsibility for managing products. It is a central task for many marketing professionals and one that can give great success to an organisation and a great sense of achievement to an individual. However, as with most responsibilities, it is also

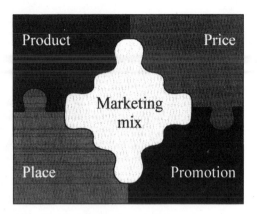

Figure 5.1 *Marketing mix showing how Ps are interlinked*

a major source of headaches. Always remember that the customer gains value from the benefits your products offer. A common mistake is to simply list features in sales literature. It's not enough – you must tell your customers how you can help them!

What is a product?

The starting point for understanding a product and how to manage it is to break it down into smaller parts and to build its profile back up again to gain a deeper understanding of what you are really dealing with.

At its simplest, a product consists of two key components: *tangible factors* – factors that can be seen and/or touched such as its physical features; and *intangible factors* – the power and strength of the brand, quality of the materials, customer care, etc. You can't see or touch these factors; nevertheless they enhance the 'product offering' to the customer.

Identifying these two components can be difficult because the emphasis we place on them differs from product to product. For example, an Armani branded scarf will probably have more emphasis and resource devoted to maintaining the brand integrity (intangible component) than say an Asda own-label tin of baked beans, where the emphasis may be on the quality and taste of the actual product (tangible component). What's important here is that both the tangible and intangible components need to work together and complement each other. For example, based upon what the Armani brand stands for in terms of price and quality, the physical scarf should also reach the required level of quality and usability deemed suitable by the intangible component of the brand.

As usual, we can break these two components down further to understand even more about the anatomy of our products.

Anatomy of a product

The core product

The core product usually refers to the actual benefit the customer derives from consuming the product, for example, the core benefit for anybody purchasing a new car is transport.

The tangible product

The tangible product is where the focus is given to the physical features and unique selling point of the actual product. For example, for a Dyson vacuum cleaner, the cyclone technology and the bagless scenario are key tangible features of the product.

The augmented product

Augmentation in this sense refers to the added value that many marketers build into their products, such as the warranty, credit terms, after-sales advice and customer service. In many respects, this is a highly competitive area and requires much thought. Indeed research has shown that 80 per cent of failure to achieve repeat business from customers is attributed to factors in the product's augmented level.

Because products are highly visible it's easy to 'copy' or 'imitate' (legally of course!) the physical features of a product from a competitive point of view. However, when it comes to augmentation, this is where an organisation can really start to differentiate itself in a more sophisticated sense that is not as visual and therefore not as easy to replicate.

The future product

When developing new products or managing existing products it is also wise to consider the future. This harks back to the definition highlighted in Chapter 1. Part of a marketer's responsibility is to consider the future and, as the world evolves and customer needs and wants change, there is often a need to transform and alter the existing product in a bid to 'move with the times'. There are different approaches to doing this success-fully, which will be discussed later.

By breaking a product down into these levels it provides a clearer view and understanding of the key issues that require consideration and resource. It's particularly useful to break products down in this way if you are new to managing prod-ucts or have inherited a portfolio of products to manage. Using this technique will help you gain a deeper understanding of the product, rather than purely accepting a product and its features at face value.

Classification of products

What we also need to be aware of from a product management perspective is how our customers purchase and behave towards them. Earlier we considered various consumer behaviour theo-ries. From a product perspective, we also need to understand how we 'classify' our products. If we can understand the classification we will gain a better understanding of how and why our customers behave towards the product. This knowledge helps us to determine not just the amount of resource required to support the customer in reaching a purchase decision, it also helps us determine the actual types of support required.

The B2C market

In a consumer market the products can be 'classed' in the following ways.

Convenience goods
These are goods that require little time on the part of the consumer when purchasing them, primarily because there is no or little risk financially, socially or personally associated with these goods. Examples are staple foods such as vegetables, bread and eggs. The customer will usually purchase these products through 'routine' or sheer habit.

Shopping goods
These require a little more time and effort by the consumer when purchasing them as they do incur an element of risk financially, personally and socially, for example a new kitchen suite or a new washing machine. This class of product would be associated with solving their 'limited' problems (see Chapter 3).

Speciality goods
These, as the name suggests, are more luxurious goods that consumers will often save up for and accept no substitutes. There is a great risk involved with these goods as they are often expensive. Branding is particularly important here, for example designer clothing and expensive perfumes such as Chanel.

Unsought goods
These are goods that consumers don't realise they require until they are drawn to their attention, for example offers for double

glazing being drawn to the attention of consumers via phone calls, or it could be through unforeseen events. Should you arrive home to find yourself standing in a foot of water in the kitchen, you may require new pipes, carpets, ceilings, etc; these would be unsought goods.

So, if you are currently responsible for a portfolio of products, into which class do they fit? Understanding the classification will highlight how consumers purchase your products and what factors are particularly important.

The B2B market

The same can be said for the business/industrial market where we 'classify' the products in the following ways.

Installations
These are the central pieces of equipment, machinery, technology, etc that are used in the production process. They are critical to the process and can be very expensive.

Accessories
These are also part of the production process but not necessarily central to it. Rather they complement it and help create a smoother process, for example, office furniture.

Raw materials
Without basic raw materials, consumer products would not be produced. The quality and timeliness of raw materials are incredibly important here.

What is meant by timely?

Well, consider the production planning team at Nintendo. They'd scheduled to ramp up production to 1.5 million Wii consoles per month in the run up to Christmas 2007. If the raw materials required to produce the consoles arrived late at the factory this could have had a dramatic effect on the production schedule and the whole campaign. Machinery, equipment and people are scheduled as effectively and efficiently as possible. If the final product to customers such as Currys and Comet arrives late, serious damage can be done to the relationship – not very effective customer service! As it was the Wii had (arguably) the most successful games console launch in history.

Services
This includes services such as cleaning.

You may find yourself marketing heavy duty production equipment or you may work for an organisation that manufactures rivets. The process for understanding your product is the same as a consumer based product. Split the product into the two components, tangible and intangible, and then split the product down into the different anatomical levels. Take this understanding further by then trying to classify your products and this will help develop your understanding of the product and also how and why customers purchase it.

So that is how and why we classify products. Now we need to look at one of the central theories governing product management, 'the product life cycle' or PLC.

The product life cycle

The PLC is named as such because products, just like human beings, have a life. This is quite a traditional concept but one that still has value. Products are conceived and developed, they are born, they grow up, mature and age and usually fall into decline (an exception being Cadbury's Dairy Milk, which has sold in largely the same format for over a hundred years). Therefore, it's important for those of us managing our products to understand how the life and age of a product affect our business and the marketplace as they, in turn, affect how we undertake additional marketing-related activities.

Figure 5.2 shows a typical representation of how a product lives its life. Let's have a look in more detail. As you can see there are five key stages to the life of a product.

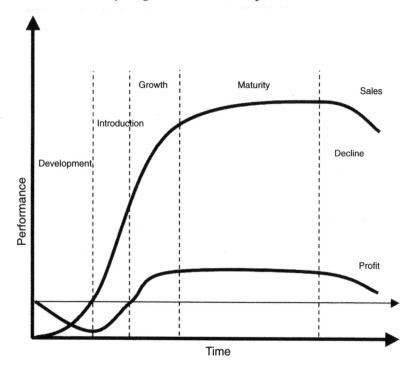

Figure 5.2 *The generic product life cycle (PLC)*

1. Development

This is where we develop ideas or concepts and invest in them through research to see if they have any value. The product hasn't been launched yet so there are no sales but as can be seen, there is a financial burden. Why? Because at this stage there is a huge investment in research, development, testing, communication, market analysis and building product proto-types. As the product hasn't been launched, it isn't generating any return, so the product at this stage is running at a loss.

2. Introduction

If the research, testing and trials are successful it may be decided to launch the product into the marketplace. As you can see, there are sales, but they are low – it often takes time for awareness of new products to filter through. However, although there are some sales, this product is still running at a loss. This is because although the product has been launched and some return is being generated, not enough products have been sold to cover all the initial costs incurred in the development stage.

3. Growth

Eventually, consumers will see and hear about this product and when they do the product will experience a huge growth spurt. Look at how steep the sales line is. The steepness of the line here not only represents huge growth but also rapid growth. And, for the first time, a profit is being generated. All the initial development costs have been recovered, creating a break-even situation and the product is now holding its own in the marketplace and making money. Phew – the sleepless nights are over (for now anyway)!

4. Maturity

However, in time the product will reach the maturity stage in its life. The product has been on the market for some time now and, dare we suggest, it is growing old. Look how the sales line flattens out. Although sales are still fairly high, they have started to slow down. Why? Because newer, more contemporary, competitive products have now entered the market. Oh yes, the competition has arrived and are now competing ferociously. However, profits are still fairly healthy. Also, have a look at the length of time the product spends in this stage of its life. According to the theory, products spend most of their life in the maturity stage.

5. Decline

There will come a time when the market conditions change to such an extent that the product starts to slip into decline. Competition is much stronger with younger and fresher products and you have to make some quite serious decisions. Do you stay in the market with this old product and milk it for all it's worth? Do you really want to be spending precious time, money and other resources on an old product when you could be spending it on creating a newer, more competitive product? Or are you going to withdraw the product from the market gracefully? This very difficult decision is yours.

Extending the life of the product

Some marketers may try to extend the maturity stage of the product's life as their new products may not be quite ready to launch and there are a number of different strategies you can try to achieve this.

Re-launch the product

Perhaps update the product slightly with a new colour or new packaging to give it a new lease of life; see Figure 5.3.

Find new uses for your product

Silk was used in the early 1900s primarily as the key raw material in the manufacture of parachutes. An alternative use was found for this product, namely silk stockings and other clothing.

Example: Lucozade was once seen as a drink for ailing older people. Now rebranded, after a re-launch featuring Daley Thomson and phrases such as 'isotonic', it's the health drink for young athletes and sports people. This not only extended

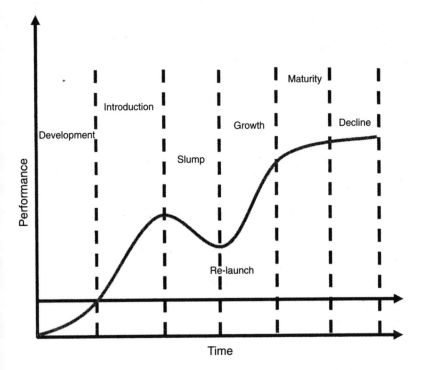

Figure 5.3 *PLC with re-launch pattern*

the maturity section but massively increased sales. It is distributed intensively (more on this in Chapter 6) and is highly visible. Many vending machines in university campuses supply Lucozade, which wouldn't have happened without the re-launch.

Find new users for your product

Rather than continuing to target a particular segment of customers can you find any others? What about international markets? Many people now take aspirins because of its blood thinning properties rather than simply curing a headache.

Increase the usage/frequency of purchase

Have a look the next time you go shopping at how many shampoos are now for 'frequent' use. If people use your product more often, they will buy more! Again, relate the benefits of your products to the customers – tell them how it helps.

Is the PLC a useful theory?

The PLC can be useful, particularly for planning and analytical purposes. It also gives us the understanding that as with a human being, as a product grows and matures, the way we manage its life requires different formulas and different approaches to support it though its journey.

However, it does have a number of limitations that need to be kept in mind when using it. It's a gross oversimplification of the real life of a product. Consider the following.

Staging

First, it is particularly difficult to understand when a product moves from one stage to another. Yes, you can check the sales and profitability data, but there are a whole host of reasons for seeing increases or decreases in those. Imagine if you are responsible for marketing a product that suffers from 'seasonality'. As soon as the sales and level of profitability start to dip, this could be taken as a transfer from maturity to decline, but what if it's merely a seasonal blip? You could end up taking action on the product that is not required or is quite inappropriate.

The shape

Look at the shape of the theoretical PLC. Again, in reality, many products do not follow this pattern. There are products that have no maturity such as 'fad' products (see Figure 5.4) – here today and gone tomorrow; there are those that have a series of 'mini' life cycles, due to the input of further new technology into the product to update it, such as the television.

External factors

The product life cycle is also a somewhat inward and myopic theory. It neglects to take into consideration any external factor such as the macro environment, customers' changing needs or the competition.

So, the PLC is a flawed theory, but – it does give us that all important starting point of truly understanding that a product does have finite life and that how we manage it through its life requires attention and skill.

To gain entry to a market with a brand new product or indeed an existing product we need to recover all of the development costs, break even as quickly as possible and move to capture profitability. Generally speaking, the PLCs of many products today are getting shorter and shorter, primarily due to fast-paced change that is fuelled by evolving technology.

Example: A consultancy client who sells hubs and routers to the key UK Internet Service Providers (ISPs) argues that PLCs for his goods are now less than 12 months and approaching six months in some cases. This highlights the need for good relationships with clients based on regular, quality communication (which we'll discuss in Chapter 8) because a disgruntled client could simply skip a generation of products. Imagine the potential impact on the router supplier's cash-flow!

So, there is a need to enter and penetrate the market quickly, raise awareness rapidly and capture the hearts and minds of the customer before the competition does. A technique that has helped marketing practitioners over the years is the product adoption process.

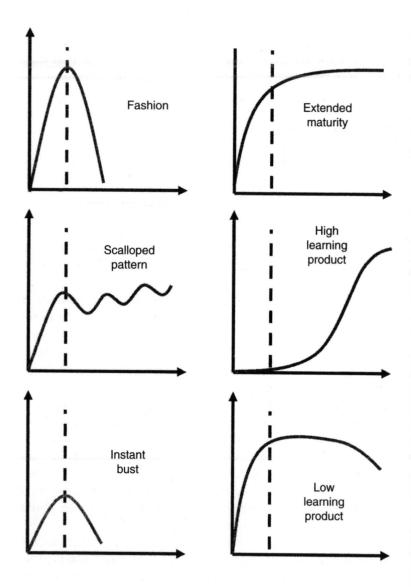

Figure 5.4 *Other PLC profiles*

The product adoption process

This process attempts to explain how a product can be 'adopted ' or 'diffused' (spread) throughout a marketplace efficiently. Consumers are sorted into a number of different categories, namely innovators, early adopters, early majority, late majority and laggards. Let's consider these in more detail.

Innovators

These tend to be young, professional, affluent, open-minded and keen to experience new things. They are opinion leaders and are influential people socially, open and willing to try new things – they aren't afraid to take a risk.

Early adopters

These adopters are similar in profile to the innovators but don't tend to have the same social standing and therefore are not as influential.

Early majority

Tend to be slightly older than the previous two categories and do not tend to have the same high income. They therefore are not as influential and do not have the social standing the others represent.

Late majority

Adopt products because they have generally been accepted by others. Social issues and economic circumstances play a part here.

Laggards

These adopters tend to be the oldest out of all the categories. They are not risk takers by nature or by any stretch of the imagination. These people really tend to sit on the fence and watch others adopt products and only when they feel the products are solidly tried and tested will they venture forth to purchase them.

This theory shows that you can identify different levels and types of adopters in the marketplace. You can use them to 'diffuse' your product appropriately into the market as quickly as possible.

Example: Publishers of academic textbooks don't communicate directly with the 1.2 million students in UK higher education as it would be far too expensive. What they do is target lecturers instead. If a lecturer adopts a book for a particular subject, it becomes a core book for the module and exam and many students will go and purchase it. The publisher is using the lecturer (an innovator) who has some degree of influence and social standing to help 'diffuse' the product throughout the marketplace. The publisher has only had to target one person to potentially reach hundreds!

So, that's the basis of issues to consider when managing your products. What is needed now is to understand how new products are developed, which is the focus of the next section of this chapter.

Developing new products

Now you have a deeper understanding of how we can recognise and manage our products, it is necessary to consider how new products are developed and the reasons for new product development (NPD).

The first thing to remember about developing new products is that there are different types of what we can term 'new' products.

Different types of new products

Innovative products

These 'products are completely and radically new to the market – nothing has been seen like it before. The television back when it was first introduced would have been innovative. It's pretty rare to see the introduction of innovative products these days. The pharmaceutical/bio-technology industries are really the key places at the moment where these new products originate. A great deal of research, development, testing, resource and time will have been spent on creating and developing 'new' products. They are initially high risk ventures, but the returns can be phenomenal. Likewise, if they fail once launched into the marketplace, they can have a devastating impact on the investing organisation.

Replacement products

Older products are updated, given a new lease of life and re-launched back onto the market with a fresh appeal. As stated earlier, as products mature they can quickly start to look tired, particularly if the product is related to fashion trends, whether it be colour based or design (size, weight etc), or if technology is central to the product. A more inexpensive way to create a 'new' product compared to the previous type is to update an existing product. There is also much less risk associated with this approach and generally it will be less resource-intensive.

Imitative products

Products, based on the idea of another, are produced and launched onto the market. Dyson launched the first mass market 'bagless' vacuum cleaner with cyclone technology. Not long after, Hoover and Electrolux also launched their bagless versions. Again, what it is interesting is that organisations can sit back and wait for other companies to invest in innovations or new approaches to a product and then 'imitate' it once it is launched. Again, this lowers the amount of risk involved in developing the new product – why incur huge risks and costs? Why not allow your competitor to do it instead? The payoff here is that if the new product is successful, rather than being the first in the market to capture the hearts and minds of the customer, you may be second or third with an imitative product, and you tend to become a 'follower' rather than a leader. You also need to be aware of legislative issues such as copyright and trademark laws.

Why do we need to create 'new' products?

As stated before, the world, the market and the needs of the customer are continually changing. Therefore there is a continuous need to create the products the market wants. Consider the television. Imagine how it looked and the technology used to produce programmes, say, in the 1950s. Televisions today look very different and have many alternative features to those of 50 years ago. If companies produced the original version today, it probably wouldn't satisfy many people and the company would go out of business.

The same can be said of mobile technology. Consider how the first mobile telephones looked and how much they cost. They were the size and weight of a brick! Now jump forward 20 years and consider how the technology has changed the size, weight, design and use of mobile technology. If organisations that produced mobile telephones in the 1980s still produced and churned out the same products today – they simply wouldn't survive.

The development and launch of new products can create great success stories for organisations and give a real sense of achievement to those involved in their conception and development. Successful new products can:

■ enhance an organisation's reputation and standing in the marketplace;
■ bring prominence to the brand;
■ increase turnover, profit and market share;
■ enhance customer satisfaction and build loyalty.

It's worth stating (what may seem obvious) that satisfied customers tend to not only stay loyal but tell others as well, stimulating and bringing new customers to the product and brand.

As the development of new products is so very risky, a systematic process is required to guide all personnel involved in the process, which in some organisations can range from one or two to several hundred. Therefore it needs to be controlled in a scientific and systematic way.

The new product development process

To try and reduce the number of failed new products, organisations have found it useful to create a systematic framework or process in which they develop them. By being more systematic and processed in your approach to developing new products, you will reduce your exposure to risk and get products to market more quickly. This process includes a number of key steps and is called the 'new product development process' or NPD; see Figure 5.5. Let's have a look at each step in the most basic process.

Figure 5.5 *New product development process*

1. Idea generation

Ideas for new products can come from within, research findings, brainstorming committees, formal NPD groups internally, even from the general public. At this stage in the process you need to develop lots of ideas, no matter how wild they may seem at the time. Really brainstorm ideas. Don't necessarily think realistically at this stage – don't limit yourself, be as wild and weird as you see fit.

2. Idea screening

This is an important step in the process. Having developed many ideas in the idea generation stage, you then need to start screening them. Which are the most commercially appropriate ideas and which are totally wild and completely inappropriate? Which ideas warrant further investigation? Which are so wild that you need to discard them? If you believe that there are a few key, commercially viable ideas at this stage, then proceed to the next step.

3. Concept testing

By now you may have one or two ideas you believe to be innovative, creative and potentially commercially successful. This next step involves testing these 'concepts' and embarking on the first round of research. Focus groups are generally a great help here. You could take mocked-up pictures of the products and ask your target audience what they think of the idea/concept, the shape, colour, design, how much they would be willing to pay for it, and where they would go to purchase it. As with any stage in this process, if the feedback is negative, you must abort.

There is no point flogging the idea of a new product if your target audience are not on board. You may decide to go back to the drawing board to redevelop your ideas, or you could drop the process altogether if the concept was received negatively. Again, this is an area where many organisations go wrong. Despite receiving negative feedback, many marketers decide to pursue the development to the next stage because they believe they are right. Avoid ritualistic or historical pressures, ie 'We've always done it this way' (the refrain of many companies that go under).

You proceed in the face of negative feedback at your peril. Do not ignore what your customer says to you. If your product concepts are received warmly, then you will have received some sound data upon which to move to the next step in the process.

4. Business analysis
This is where the number crunching starts. How much would it cost to produce these products? Does there need to be an investment in any capital equipment? What is the size of the market, how many of these products do we think we can sell and at what price? Who are the competitors? What products will yours be competing against? A great deal of analytical and forecasting work will be undertaken at this stage. Typically this is the first time price is seriously considered. What margins do we wish to make? Basically, do the numbers add up and present you with a winning situation? If they don't, you need to stop the process now and look at other ideas.

Again, it may be difficult to break off the process at this stage, particularly as you've hit on a key concept that has been warmly received. But remember, it is a tough world out there and you have to ensure that the product is financially and commercially sound and will work in the marketplace and wider environment. However, if your new product idea seems commercially viable and marketable, continue to the next step.

5. Product development
At this stage you will develop prototypes of the product and start testing them. Production will be tooling up and quality teams will be getting even more involved. You may put these prototypes into research to see what potential customers think about it. Focus groups are particularly useful as they can actually start to touch, use and feel the product's physical prototypes. This feedback can be crucial to the successful product launch.

In parallel with developing the prototypes, you should be designing the entire marketing strategy behind the product, namely the selling price, the distribution channels to get the product to the customer, the packaging and additional communication tools. All of these issues can be checked out in the focus groups. Have you hit the correct price point, particularly when compared to the competition? Do the customers respond to the packaging if it plays a central role in the purchasing process? If the feedback is negative, stop the process. If it is positive, continue to the next step.

6. Test marketing
This is where you test out the launch of the product with its complete marketing strategy, namely the actual product and packaging; its price in the outlets through which you intend it to be distributed; its branding; and how it's perceived compared to competitors. The test market is usually undertaken in a geographically controlled area, usually a town or city and the marketers watch to see what they can learn from the 'test'. Are the products selling as anticipated? Have they got the price of the product correct? Has the packaging fulfilled its intended functions?

What you are doing is using a test market to 'test' your entire marketing strategy. It is a safety net situation. If feedback from the test is negative in any way this gives you time to address the problems before the full launch of your product.

However, you have to be cautious if you use a test market. Although it is a great safety net device before going to full launch, the trade off is that your competitors may find out where you are 'testing', and could cause problems and have a good look at your product back at their labs. They could potentially start tweaking their own products and launch very quickly against you, creating a highly competitive environment.

7. Product launch
If your test market has been successful and you truly believe that the product, its price, distribution and communication are

all correct, you will then roll out your new products into the actual marketplace.

It is crucial that if the feedback from any of the stages is negative, you stop the process. As you continue through the process, the development costs and associated risks start to increase.

However, even though a large number of organisations now use a process such as the one above to develop new products, many new products still fail. Why? Because although the system above is systematic and designed to try to eliminate the risks involved, there is still a lot of judgement needed – and skill. Again, you may want to seek support from third parties at various points in the NPD process.

As you move through this process, it can take weeks, months and in some cases, years to complete and as we are aware, the environment, marketplace and customer are constantly evolving. This is difficult to manage as the goalposts seem to be constantly moving.

NPD is not an easy situation to manage but it can be extremely rewarding if successful. Now you have an overview of the process, let's consider some of the main risks involved.

The risks involved in NPD

NPD is central to successful marketing and enterprise; however it can be an extremely risky venture, financially, professionally and personally. An alarming number of new products fail.

Armstrong and Kotler (2007) refer to research that shows that, of 34,000 new consumer food, beverage, beauty and healthcare products launched, less than 2 per cent were considered successful. They cite another study that estimates that new consumer packaged products fail at a rate of 90 per cent within two years.

These are sobering statistics in one sense but understandable in another. One area of general business practice that is often prone to failure is indeed new product development and the reasons for it are, at times, evident.

Why do new products fail so often?

New products fail for a variety of reasons. Let's consider some in detail.

Lack of market research

Many organisations fail to undertake the initial investment in research. Why? Because it is often time-consuming, resource-intensive and expensive. Large organisations tend to have the resources available, but many smaller organisations don't, so they rely on gut feel and current knowledge. To a certain extent gut feel should not be ignored, especially if you have a lot of experience in the field and market you are targeting. However, common sense also has to be used. Can you really make empathetic decisions on behalf of what could be potentially millions of customers? You need to ensure that the research carried out throughout the process is collected and analysed correctly. Again, this is an area where many organisations fall down. Collecting the data is one thing, but has the data been analysed and interpreted correctly? Remember, if the data presented and analysed is flawed, the decisions you make based upon it also risk being flawed.

Inappropriate forecasting and planning

Many organisations also fail to forecast and plan accordingly throughout the new product development process. Forecasting and projecting sales and turnover is not easy, particularly if you are entering markets of which you have little or no experience, but many organisations are over-zealous with their future plans. Be realistic, don't create targets you can't hope to attain. This is particularly problematic if investment is secured against planned targets.

Poor NPD management

Another key reason for NPD failure is purely down to the mismanagement of the NPD process. Many organisations don't seem to have a central system that is applied to NPD; rather they stumble and fumble from one aspect to another. This can lead quite easily to communication breakdown, missed information and a whole host of meltdown situations.

Key points

- For customers to buy products we have to develop, make and manage them.
- A product is more complex than initially thought and it is formed from both tangible and intangible factors.
- Consumer products can be categorised into the following classes: convenience goods, shopping goods, speciality goods, and unsought goods.
- Industrial products can be categorised into the following classes: installations, accessories, component parts, raw materials, services.
- The product life cycle (PLC) is a traditional theory that highlights the fact that a product has a life: it is developed, it is introduced to the market, it grows more successful, matures and finally declines.
- Although the PLC is useful as a means to understand what additional activities a product needs to support it through its life, it also has its limitations. The concept is an oversimplification of reality, it is difficult to determine exactly what stage a product is in and the concept ignores the external environment.
- The product adoption/diffusion cycle is useful as it shows how a marketer can target only one or two subsets of customers in the marketplace, who will in turn help diffuse the product and get it accepted amongst the majority of potential customers.
- Developing new products and launching them into the marketplace can help organisations remain competitive, increase profitability, sales, market share and customer satisfaction and loyalty.
- Developing new products can also be an extremely risky venture. Financial losses, a loss of reputation, image, customer satisfaction and loyalty can all occur if the product fails.

- ■ To try to reduce the number of failed products, a range of screening processes have been developed.
- ■ The new product development process is the screening process that systematically leads the marketer through a more controlled and organised process of developing new ideas and subsequent products, allowing them to abort the development at any stage if the feedback is at all negative. This helps to reduce the financial investment in the process and hopefully the embarrassing failure of launching a product that nobody wants.

Activities

Look at the vast array of products you have purchased for your home. Start to classify them. Are they convenience products, shopping goods, specialist goods, were they unsought? Link this back to how you purchased them (Chapter 3). Did you move through the consumer buying process when you purchased these products? How quickly? Was risk involved? Have a think about any products you have had to replace. How long did you have the original? How has the new product been updated from the original?

Now, try to classify your organisation's products and link them back to the customer purchasing them.

Get hold of a normal household product and place it in front of you. Imagine you are developing a newer, fresher version of it. Using the NPD process, write down just what is involved in each of the steps you would take.

Questions

1. Why do marketers need to be able to classify their products?
2. What is meant by the 'intangible' component of a product?
3. What is generally happening to the length of PLCs? What are the consequences of this?
4. Identify three different strategies you can use to extend the life of your product.
5. How can products be diffused quickly through the marketplace?

Right time, right place, right quantity, right condition

What do we mean by 'place'?

Place is one of the 4Ps (part of the marketing mix) and refers to how an organisation gets the right product to the right place in the right quantity, in the right condition at the right time. Place is about marketing channels and distribution/logistics, and is just as important in a business-to-business environment as it is in a business-to-consumer market.

Have you, as a customer, saved your money to purchase a specific product or service, gone to the store to purchase it only to be told 'Sorry, we're out of stock'? What about buying something, getting it home, unwrapping all the packaging only to find that it's damaged or there are pieces missing?

If you work for a business that places orders for deliveries from other organisations, how often do they fail to deliver on time or with the correct number of items delivered?

The role and importance of place

The role and importance of place has grown in significance over the years for a number of different reasons. A great deal of money is spent on getting the products to the right place at the right time. Wherever costs are high, there is always potential for savings. If your company ships goods, try to find out just how much it costs to get your products from A to B. This is particularly important if you factor products in from overseas. If you are purchasing space on container vessels, wagons, or trains, whatever the mode of transport, there are inevitable costs, financial and logistical.

As more and more organisations turn to the Far East for manufactured goods, the process of how to logistically manoeuvre the freight half way around the world to markets in the West has increased in importance and significance.

Example: When it goes awry it can be costly, as Microsoft discovered when its supply chain couldn't ship enough Xbox 360 consoles into the EU for the Christmas 2006 launch. It resorted to 'flying in' units from China. Its willingness to meet the customer demand is laudable, but the disruption to the planned delivery method had financial and environmental implications.

This area of the marketing arena can really affect the level of satisfaction of a customer. From a B2B perspective, if your suppliers fail to deliver your orders on time and in the correct quantity and quality, the chances are you will look for an alternative source. Alternatively, if you as the customer fail to continually deliver customers' orders on time and with insufficient quantity and quality, the chances are you will be dropped pretty quickly.

Most organisations today operate in a highly competitive domain, so if you are incapable of performing to high standards there are others who can and will win your orders away from you. Simply put, this area of 'place' can help you achieve a competitive advantage. If you actually carry out what you state you will, deliver on time in the right numbers and quality and provide excellent customer service, the chances are you will start to win the confidence and trust of your customers. It is surprising how many times organisations fail to deliver on their promises.

To try to understand 'place' further, it's easier to split it down into two sections: marketing channels and distribution logistics. Let's first consider marketing channels.

Marketing channels

Basically, they are the channels through which your products reach your customers and there are a number of different ways this can be done. Channel design is important and there is a need to have a look at some of the key factors to be considered when designing a marketing channel; see Figure 6.1.

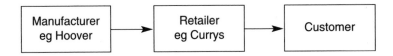

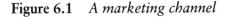

Figure 6.1 *A marketing channel*

One of the first considerations is how long the channel is going to be. Do you want to distribute your product directly to the customer or indirectly? Direct distribution has been augmented by the use of new technologies to such an extent that a wide range of organisations now sell direct. An example of this is recording artists bypassing the retailers and shipping direct (see www.xtcidearecords.co.uk for a good example).

A company may choose to distribute its product to its customer directly. This is often known as a 'zero level' channel as there are no (zero) other businesses involved in getting your product to the customer. This is a method, as the closer you are to your customers, the better. You will get to know your customers, start forming a relationship with them, receive timely feedback and, perhaps even more important, you will retain control over how your product reaches the customer and the entire marketing strategy.

Using an intermediary is a one-level channel (see Figure 6.2) because there's only one level (another business) between the manufacturer and customer. An intermediary helps move the product through the channel so it becomes available to the right customer. Intermediaries can be a retailers, wholesalers, agents or franchisors.

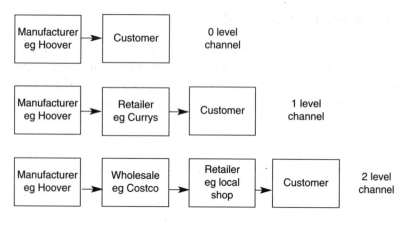

Figure 6.2 *0, 1 and 2 level channels*

Why use an intermediary?

There are many reasons. For example, retailers and wholesalers already have an established network of outlets to reach a certain set of customers. That is why many organisations such as Heinz use retailers, like Tesco, to sell their products. If Heinz had to reach its customers directly, establishing its own network of stores would cost millions. Why not use an existing network of stores that are already established in the market-place?

Convenience is also an important factor. As well as using existing retailers and therefore, using somebody else's resource (saving you lots of money!) you are also providing your customer with further convenience. A retailer such as Tesco has stores in most cities and towns in the UK. Your customer hasn't far to travel to reach your product.

If your organisation is not primarily involved in retail, for example if you work for a manufacturing organisation, leave the retailing to the experts. Let the wholesalers get on with wholesaling, leaving you, your time and resources focusing on what you do best. Use the existing pool of skills, knowledge and resources to the best of your ability.

You can also have a two-level channel (see Figure 6.2). This where there are two intermediaries between the manufacturer and customer. Some manufacturing organisations will sell their products to a large wholesaler. Smaller retailers then buy their products from the larger wholesalers and sell them in their stores to the end-user.

So, when it comes to channel design you have a number of choices to make. Do you prefer a shorter or longer marketing channel? Do you wish to distribute your products directly or indirectly? Key factors affecting these choices include costs, convenience, customer requirements and control.

The longer your channel, the further removed you generally are from the end-user. Imagine you work for a manufacturing organisation and you have designed a two-level channel. Gaining immediate feedback from the consumer market is not an easy task. Generally speaking, if a customer has a problem with your product, he or she takes it back to the retailer with their complaint. The retailer in turn complains to the wholesaler and then, eventually, the complaint will be filtered back to you in the manufacturing organisation.

You can also potentially lose aspects of control over your marketing strategy. You may have undertaken research in the consumer market to deduce what price point you need to hit, how it should be positioned in the marketplace, etc. However, you can't dictate these points to your intermediaries. As soon as they pay for their order from you, they take title of the product and ultimately control.

This then brings the strength of your relationship into the spotlight. If you truly intend to use intermediaries in your channel, they can offer you great skill, resources and expertise and can share risks. However, from a long-term perspective, you should view them not just as intermediaries, but as partners in your business.

You may work for a successful manufacturing organisation that has great skill, resources and knowledge, but if you can't get your product to market, you have no business. Alternatively, you may work for a retailer, again with great flair and experience in its field, but if you have no product to sell in your outlets, you have no business. You need each other. Time and resource needs spending on developing and strengthening your relationship. Trust and confidence should be central to a long-term relationship, but that is easier said than done. If you choose to design and use a one- or two-level channel, conflict must be avoided at all costs – again, this is easier said than done.

It is due to this potential loss of control, lack of immediate feedback and reliance on other organisations, that there has been growth in direct distribution. With the development of the internet and other related digital technologies, many organisations have turned to using their own retail stores or selling online. However, although websites can be created to attract customers and facilitate their purchasing, you still need to develop and maintain an effective delivery system to customers to achieve complete satisfaction. Making it easy for customers to order products from the comfort of their home may be a key advantage, but if the delivery service fails to get goods to them on time and in one piece, you can lose customers.

Market coverage

Once you have decided upon the length of the channel and whether you intend to use intermediaries or not, you also need to consider the amount of market coverage you require for your product.

Broadly speaking you have three distribution strategic choices: exclusive, intensive or selective distribution. Let's consider each of these.

Exclusive distribution

This is where you purposefully limit the availability of your product to the market, which affords an image of exclusivity. For example, you don't find Aston Martin cars being sold in every town or city in the UK. The product is purposefully limited in its availability to emphasise its exclusive appeal.

Intensive distribution

This is the complete opposite of exclusive distribution. This strategy is often used by companies distributing convenience and 'habitual use' products such as toilet rolls, milk and potatoes. A wide spread of distribution (intensive coverage) is required as customers often need these products on a daily basis. Availability and convenience are key issues to consider here.

Selective distribution

This lies somewhere between intensive and exclusive distribution. You require good coverage for your product but not to the extent of the intensive approach or limited availability as with the exclusive approach. You wish to select certain key stores to distribute your product. Organisations distributing televisions and CD players use this particular strategy.

If you decide to use an indirect approach to your distribution (using intermediaries) it is always useful to establish a solid relationship with the intermediaries and determine who does what. This ensures that the channel runs smoothly; conflict within the channel between intermediaries can lead to real problems.

Terms, tasks and responsibilities

One of the key sources of conflict is lack of communication and 'stepping on other's toes'. So, clearly define the roles, terms and relationships early on.

Distribution logistics

This part of 'place' refers to the practical realities of how we physically move products from one place to another. There are a number of issues that need to be considered.

Transport

Products can be transported using air freight, cargo ships, railways, lorries, cars, motorbikes.... A lot of time and effort needs to be given to deciding how you are going to transport your products from one intermediary to another. Costs, convenience and ability all need to be taken into account.

The role of packaging is also important here as damaged goods are often a source of complaint. The packaging needs to be robust enough to withstand the journey and the mode of transport used.

Warehousing

Many organisations store products in warehouses and as they receive orders, the products are picked from the appropriate location in the warehouse, put on board transport and delivered to the customer. Where you locate your warehouses and how many you have is a key decision. Again, this can be a costly venture. A lot of thinking needs to go into how many and where the warehouses are to be located.

Order processing

In a B2B situation an order processing system is usually required. This system also wraps itself around inventory management. Stock is costly, particularly if it is finished goods sitting in a warehouse. Costs in terms of insurance and security start to increase at this stage. Stock needs to be converted into sales quickly to create income and liquidity for the business.

However, how you manage your stock is not an easy task, particularly today. If a key client approaches you to fulfil an order quickly and you don't have the stock, the chances are you will have to let them down, causing the customer to go to a competitor. Alternatively, you may decide to hold some stock to accommodate any rush orders that may arise, particularly at peak periods. However, if those 'rush' orders never materialise, your stock will start costing you money.

Organisation and time management are crucial skills in this area of marketing and you will need to work closely with the warehouse and production management teams. Why? Because, quite simply, if orders fail to materialise based upon contracted or promised terms, customer dissatisfaction will follow, and they will look to your competitors to furnish their orders instead. The same can be said in the B2C market. There is so much competition and choice out there for the customer, if you don't satisfy them, your competitors will.

Key points

- The role of place is particularly important and is involved with getting the right products to the right place at the right time in the right condition. Failure to do so can result in customer dissatisfaction.
- There are two key points to consider when studying place: marketing channels and physical logistics.
- Decisions as to whether to use intermediaries or not are important.

■ Key reasons why intermediaries are often used include: they are skilled, have knowledge and there is an existing resource, saving you money and time.

■ A number of organisations prefer to distribute directly (zero-level channel) for the following reasons: more control, being closer to the customer, easier to elicit feedback from the customer, often lowers price to consumer (cutting out the middleman) and further flexibility.

■ Logistics includes decisions relating to warehousing: number, size and location, transport, internal ordering systems, etc.

Activities

Go to your kitchen cupboard and pull out six items. Can you trace where you bought them from? Did you buy them direct? If so, why? What advantages were there for you in shopping this way? Or, did you go to a retailer, wholesaler, etc? Why do you think the companies responsible for these products/brands use these intermediaries?

Questions

1. Why has the use of direct distribution increased in recent years?
2. What are the advantages of using intermediaries in channel design?
3. With what class or type of product would an exclusive distribution strategy be used?
4. What benefits does a long channel design afford?
5. How can customer dissatisfaction materialise from this aspect of marketing?

You paid how much?

Pricing is often one of the most difficult areas for a marketer. Why? Because there are so many different factors you have to consider and (try to) balance. Pricing is also an incredibly important variable of the marketing mix to manage as:

- Price is the only variable in the marketing mix that creates revenue.
- It is of strategic importance and will be monitored closely by higher management.
- The price of a product or a service connects the customer to the supplier.
- Price also conveys a signal about quality and exclusivity to the customer and marketplace.

Get it right and you can have a successful product or service. Get it wrong and you may fail to recover initial developmental costs, make a profit, satisfy customers and compete effectively.

What factors do we need to consider when setting a price?

As mentioned earlier, pricing is probably the marketing mix tool that is often considered to be the most difficult to manage and feel comfortable with. The underlying reasons for this are many and varied. You need to manage and balance them to arrive at an actual price and pricing technique.

Price setting

When trying to set an actual price there is a large number of balancing factors that come into play, such as the following.

The customer

How much is the customer willing to pay? How much will he or she demand at a certain price? During the NPD process, you will have undertaken research (probably focus groups) and posed the question about pricing and how much the customer is willing to pay, so use this information as it should be relatively up to date and accurate.

Many marketers believe it is appropriate to make empathetic decisions on behalf of the customer – but this can be dangerous. If you are operating in a consumer market where you sell thousands of products to tens of thousands of customers, can you really make an empathetic judgement on how much they are willing to pay for a product?

Example: Could Nintendo have charged more for the Wii? Considering the huge demand (1.5 million units per month, it couldn't keep up with demand in late 2007) an extra $20 per unit would have added $360 million to the bottom line over a year's trading. When considering that its nearest competitors, Sony and Microsoft, were appreciably more expensive, it is worth remembering that it's easy to lower prices but *hard* to put them up. Nintendo is on record as judging the demand exceeding supply at launch as a missed opportunity and not a marketing 'gimmick'.

In the B2B market, the situation is slightly different as you will tend to have a closer relationship with your customers and there are usually fewer of them. However, once again, you need to take a step back. Getting the pricing correct first time is important, so consider the research initiatives you have available to you based upon your resource bank. If you can invest in research to focus on what prices your products should be then it would be a wise investment – however, as always, not all organisations have the time and resources to do this.

The competition

How good is your offering compared to the competition? Can you ask a higher price? Is your brand worth more to the customer than your competitors'?

Again, as part of the NPD process, the chances are that you will have conducted a competitor analysis to enable you to take a bird's eye view of the competition in the marketplace. Based upon your initial view of what you believe your price point is going to be, how do you sit in the marketplace alongside the competition? You need to consider your product specification and its wealth of benefits and features as well as the value of the brand and the statement you are trying to make in the market.

By placing your product on the market (on paper at this stage only) based upon its product specification, features and benefits, it will tell you how your product stands in relation to your closest competition and the price points you need to consider.

Costs

To create a product or service, costs are incurred. Quite simply, you need to cover your costs when setting a price.

Again, through the NPD process, you will have a record of the SPC (standard product cost) of your product or service and the accounts team should be keeping you up to date with any changes to this. The basic requirement of any (or most!) pricing decisions is that the price initially covers the cost of your product or service offering. You also need to work with the management team to establish the margin of profitability you need to achieve from an organisational perspective. This could be based upon the individual requirement of the product; it could be that the team try to achieve a particular margin for the range; it could be a historic judgement.

What's important is that you have a core understanding of all cost-related issues. The SPC is the tip of the iceberg; you also need to consider the product's overall development cost and the pay-back period. As discussed earlier, the length of the PLC for many products today is reducing, creating less time for you to recover all the initial development costs, cover your SPC and make a profit – not easy!

Corporate and marketing objectives

What is the organisation trying to achieve and how can the prices of your products or services help?

The pricing of your products and services should not be set separately from the current circumstances of the organisation as a whole. If you work for a small company that is struggling to survive, perhaps with a cash-flow and/or liquidity problem, manipulating your pricing can be used both strategically and tactically – perhaps being set to only just cover costs but set to compete and undercut, creating volume of sales and rapid cash-flow and liquidity for the business.

There are other factors to consider but those listed above are considered to be the 'big four'. Trying to take all these factors into consideration is difficult. Imagine that you calculate all your costs per product/service. You identify the margin you wish to make. You analyse the competition and their offerings and prices and you set a price accordingly. But what if customers aren't willing to accept the price you have set? What if they see your offering as inferior to the competition and suggest lowering prices? If you lower your price this may then put you head to head with your greatest competitor. If you price below them you may not be making the profit margin required or even cover your costs. As you can see, it can be a difficult balancing act and one often fraught with frustration.

Pricing perspectives

Many academics refer to the three perspectives of pricing: the economist, the accountant and the marketer's perspectives. These are credible from a professional point of view and can show you how pricing can be viewed by different stakeholder mindsets.

The accountant's perspective

Pricing should fall under the domain of the marketing team, but in some organisations it is still overseen by accountants. The problem with this approach is a long-term one as accountants don't monitor the marketplace, customer requirements/needs, the competition or wider environmental forces that will affect the pricing of the products and services.

However, that doesn't mean accountants are redundant in pricing matters. Indeed, they have a key role in setting correct prices and this is one of the tricks of creating a successful pricing policy. Use the personnel in the organisation to gather and offer the best information possible, so you can create the most appropriate price point at that time. Involve them in the process rather than alienating them.

Take costs as the basis of calculating a price. If you identify and calculate the total cost of producing and marketing a product or service, then you have your starting point for making a profit. For example, if it costs you £5 to produce and market one chair and your company expects you to make a 50 per cent margin on all products, you would charge £7.50 for the product. If you're not confident with numbers, then ask the accountants to help you calculate the total costs.

The economist's perspective

This takes economic theory as the basis for setting a price, founded in the forces of supply and demand. Simply put, where demand equals supply, a price will be set. However, if supply and/or demand fluctuates, then so will the price. We can see these fluctuations in the petrol market at the moment. Recent outbreaks of war, threats of terrorism and the malfunction of pipelines are affecting (perceptions of) the supply of oil and petrol. As demand is still the same, the price inevitably is being pushed higher and higher. Likewise, if there is an over-supply of certain products and/or services and demand remains the same or it falls, the price will also fall. So, if you can, try to estimate the demand for your product/service.

The marketer's perspective

This focuses more externally than the previous perspectives. The customer is the focus. How much is the customer willing to pay? Quite often, a marketer would undertake research to determine this issue, for example, using focus groups to show the prospective customer the product and its competition and asking them to determine the prices of them. It is often a useful way to get a real insight in to the mindset of the customer.

So which of the three perspectives should we use?

In reality all three perspectives offer something of value to the process. If your organisation primarily uses one of these perspectives, it could fail in the long term. Pricing is a balancing act and elements of all three perspectives should be used. You should be able to see how these three perspectives encapsulate most of the 'inputs' into pricing decisions outlined at the start of the chapter.

Different pricing techniques

Once you have a sound understanding of the cost mechanisms, the offerings you will be competing against, the requirements and willingness of the customer and the circumstances of the organisation as a whole, you then need to decide the pricing technique to be used. There is a variety of techniques that can help you price your product/service appropriately. Have a look at a few of the more common ones listed below. They each have their own advantages and disadvantages.

Cost-plus pricing

An easy and flexible technique to use. Calculate the total cost of producing one product and add the required margin to calculate the price. No skill is necessary to use this technique, but it is very inward looking, purely looking at the cost base of the product. What about the customer? Environmental factors? The competition?

Going-rate pricing

Another easy and flexible approach to pricing. Analyse the competition and their offerings and prices. If you believe that your offering is just as good as the competition and you prefer to maintain stability in the marketplace you may decide to use the 'going rate' – the price charged by your competitor(s).

However, if you believe that your offering is superior to the competition's, eg a more powerful brand name, additional features and benefits, you may decide to price above the competition. This is called 'premium pricing'. However, if after analysing the marketplace you decide that your offering is in fact inferior to the competition's, then you may decide to set a price lower than them. This is known as 'discount pricing'.

There are also two pricing techniques that focus on the marketplace and customer. These are known as 'marketing skimming' and 'market penetration' pricing. Let's have a look at these:

Market skimming

This is where you decide to enter the market with a high price and then, as the product/service matures and more innovative products are launched, you start to 'skim' the price (lower it). Many products use this approach, particularly those that incorporate technology. As discovered in Chapter 5, developing new products or services can be extremely costly, particularly those that encompass technology. The time that the manufacturer has to recover all those development and capital costs is very short, as technology changes and is updated very quickly. Think about the life cycle of a mobile telephone – it's incredibly short as new technology is continually being used to update the features.

Market penetration

This is the opposite of market skimming. This is where an organisation chooses to price its offering lower than the competition to gain entry to the marketplace. Then, as it starts to become better known, it begins to increase its prices slightly. This is a particularly useful technique if you are not particularly well known and you need to give the customer a reason to choose your product/service rather than that offered by the more established competition. It is also a useful technique to use if selling large quantities is an objective. Overall, it is a good method for penetrating a market quickly and securing a firm foothold and volume of sales.

As mentioned earlier, pricing is also a signal to customers and competitors about issues such as quality and exclusivity. It can therefore be assumed that we can affect customers 'psychologi-

'cally' with our pricing. Two such techniques are called 'odd' and 'even' pricing.

Odd and even pricing

It is claimed that customers psychologically perceive products with prices that are set at rounded figures, for example £5, £10, £100, as being better quality than those with prices set at 'odd' prices, eg £1.99, £9.99, £99.99. Next time you go to Marks and Spencer have a look at the prices. Generally speaking, it uses even prices – a mark of quality.

Odd pricing is also used as customers do tend to round down the prices when telling others, rather than rounding upwards. For example, a new pair of jeans may have cost £49.99 – often people will tell others they cost £40 rather than £50.

So, set your pricing points carefully. You'll need a great deal of information from various sources to be able to start creating the price point you wish to hit. It is a fine balancing act and you must monitor your prices constantly.

How should we check prices?

That very much depends upon the nature (and size) of your organisation and the market and environment you're operating in. Pricing is primarily used operationally to generate the revenue required and to cover all costs. However, it can be used in a much more sophisticated sense, tactically and strategically; to gain entry to markets and to create barriers to entry for others – but use it wisely.

Key points

■ Pricing has an important role to play as it is the only 'P' in the marketing mix that generates revenue; it connects customers to the point of sale and also sends many messages to customers about quality and exclusivity.

- Many factors have to be taken into consideration when setting a price: the costs, the competition, the customers' willingness to pay the price, the objectives of the organisation and marketing team, and any legal and/or regulatory issues that should be taken into account.
- There are three key pricing perspectives: the economist's, the accountant's and the marketer's perspectives. Each has its own merits and drawbacks. A marketer should consider elements of all three perspectives to set a price.
- There are many different strategies/techniques to set a price including: cost-plus pricing, going-rate pricing, premium pricing, discount pricing, market skimming, market penetration, and odd and even pricing.

Activities

Next time you're shopping have a good look at the prices of certain products and services. Consider what pricing techniques the organisation/brand is using and compare it to the competition. What factors has the organisation/brand had to take into consideration to create that particular price?

Use the leading retailers to plot a perceptual map with price and quality as the axes. It's often useful to plot a historical map of, say, 10 years ago and contrast it with the current scenario. Then if you've that extra bit of energy plot one for where they'll be in five years time. These maps can be simple but powerful tools to help plot price repositioning strategically.

Questions

1. Why is pricing such a difficult factor to compute?
2. What are the key factors that require consideration before setting a price point?
3. What role does pricing play psychologically?
4. Who should be responsible for setting a pricing policy? The marketing team or accountants? Why?

How communication works

How does marketing communication actually work?

One would think that the answer is relatively simple but, as with most things in life, understanding how marketing communication works is actually slightly more complex than most people initially believe. The word 'promotion' is useful as it nicely fits in to the 4Ps scenario. However, it can be misleading, as you'll discover later. The preferred term is 'communication'.

Over the years, marketing communication activities have increased in importance and have become a central activity in most people's lives. Whether we are the people who create and send messages to the market or those who receive (and react to) them, it's fair to say that communication activities are part and parcel of our everyday lives.

Whilst you're sat reading this book, look up and around you. How many brand names on people's clothing (including your own) can you see? Have you got the TV on in the background? Are there any adverts playing or that you've noticed? What about newspapers or magazines lying around? Are there any posters on the wall? Pop-ups on your computer if you are sat at your desk? Yes indeed, marketing messages are all around us and are here to stay.

As technology is becoming more sophisticated, so are our means of getting our messages to the relevant audience, which is why it's important to understand not just how we create our messages and get them to our audiences. Our understanding must start with appreciating just how communication works at a basic level; see Figure 8.1.

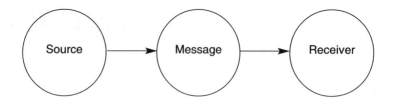

Figure 8.1 *A simple communication model*

First, we have a sender who is the party transmitting the communication. The message travels via a medium (or it can be several media). The medium is the means through which the message travels to the receiver. The receiver is the intended target for the message. Easy isn't it?

However, we can be a little more sophisticated than that. If we really understand the nature and habits of our receiver we can 'encode' the message that we are sending to them. Don't be put off by this strange word. All encoding means is that we can dress the message up with signs, symbols and language that the receiver will completely understand.

Example: If a TV advert was being designed to create awareness of a new pair of trainers for boys aged 13 to16, it would probably have boys of the same age in the advert, wearing street clothing (and the trainers, of course!) with funky music playing in the background. The message has been 'encoded' in such a way that the receiver will respond positively. It may not appeal to females or people over 30 but that wouldn't be a worry, as they aren't the target receiver.

Have you found adverts funny, but your parents, grandparents or friends can't see the humour in them? This may be due to the message being encoded in such a way that only the intended receiver can 'decode' (ie understand and interpret) the actual message and symbols in the communication. Next time you're watching TV with people, particularly of different ages, look at their reactions to different adverts. Do they respond in different ways? Can you tell from the encoding who the intended receiver is?

What is important is to understand that to encode a message correctly, so that the intended receiver can decode and respond to it appropriately, you need to closely understand your intended receiver and this is where your research skills will play a key role. However, there is something we need to be very careful of when creating and sending our messages and this 'something' is usually referred to as 'noise'; see Figure 8.2.

Noise is the bane of a communicator's life. It surrounds us and interferes with the basic communication process. The easiest way to explain noise is through a quick exercise. At some point yesterday you probably watched TV or read a

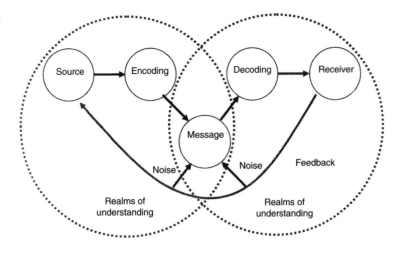

Figure 8.2 *Linear model of communication, based on Fill, 2006*

newspaper. Write down in the next 10 seconds the last advert you saw. What was the brand? What was the central message they were trying to communicate? Don't just remember a particular advert you've seen recently, write down the actual last advert you saw before going to bed last night. Struggling? You're not alone. It's an exercise that most people tend to struggle with. Why can't you remember?

The people responsible for creating and sending these ads have probably spent thousands of pounds (if not millions) trying to reach you and spent weeks, possibly months, creating and preparing the ads. The reason you can't easily remember the last ad is due to noise. This can be information overload – we are so busy with work, cooking, cleaning the house or doing the school run we can only take in so much information. We are so bombarded with information via marketing communication messages that we simply can't remember everything we see or are told. Even simple things like whether we are in a good or bad mood can affect what we see and how much we take in, what we notice and, more worryingly, what we don't.

Therefore, an additional skill and task of a good communicator is to be realistic and understand the nature of noise and create communication pieces that can snake through all the clutter that is bombarding us today, to be the key piece of communication that our receivers do actually take notice of, remember and respond to. There are lots of ways to do this. We can use music. Those who grew up through the 1980s will respond to tunes from this era. Animation, fantasy, imagery and sex are all instruments we can use to help draw attention to our piece of communication. Think about the TV ads that you like – why do you like them? What draws your attention to them? What is it about them that makes you notice them above all others? Next time you are reading a newspaper or magazine and an ad draws your attention, consider why. We'll explore this later.

What we also need to remember is that communication is a process. It isn't linear, it is a continual process. Why? Because as the world and marketplace is continually evolving and our target audience and receivers are changing around us, so do our communication activities. Our messages need updating and, as stated earlier, technology has had a profound effect on this area of marketing. The nature and means of how we get our message to our receiver has never been more exciting with the options we now have available.

Whilst today's new technologies offer exciting communications choices, there are also challenges. Whenever you create a piece of communication, whether it is a PR item, a sales promotion, an ad or direct mail letter, you must always create a mechanism that allows you to monitor, control and check whether it has worked and achieved its objectives. You may spend large amounts of time and money on your communication activities so you need to know if they're effective or not. If they are – great! But why have you got it so right? What can be taken from this success to create another? If the communication is failing, why? Is the message unclear? Is it the medium chosen to carry the message to the receiver? Is it down to noise? Is the encoding incorrect? You need to know quickly if the communication is not working and to investigate why so you don't make the same mistake twice.

When marketing communication works well it can provide untold success for the brand/company, etc. However, if it goes wrong, it can have quite devastating effects. Not only can precious time, money and resources be wasted, but brand names, brand equity (the value of the brand) and the reputation of the company can all be affected adversely. Because many of our communication activities are published external to the organisation, our mistakes are there for all to see: our intended receivers, our competitors and the media.

The two-stage communication process

As you now have an understanding of the basic communication process we can start to build upon it. To be good communicators we have to be practical and realistic. One of the key factors to take on board is that there are many influences and none is more important than the people who surround us every day.

We need to acknowledge this and remember it when we are creating, planning and executing our communication activities. When faced with making purchase decisions, particularly larger, riskier purchases, consumers often turn to materials that help provide the information needed to make the correct decision. Consumers read magazines and use the internet to glean more information and often, above all else, turn to the people around them for advice and guidance. They ask colleagues, friends, but most of all family. We can probably all recall a purchase situation that we've been through and find that despite all the sophisticated communication materials we read and researched, it was actually the advice and opinions of those closest to us that carried the most weight.

Why do we need to know about opinion leaders and opinion formers?

In some purchase situations, people turn to others for support and guidance, so when you create your marketing communication activities you may reach others who are not the intended target. If they can influence the purchase you need to draw them in so that they can support and ultimately influence the purchaser.

The terms 'opinion formers' and 'opinion leaders' are what many marketers refer to when considering the communication process and the influence certain persons can have upon it.

An *opinion former* is somebody who, usually through his or her education and profession, has expertise you listen to and respond to. Quite often, companies trying to promote a new headache or hay fever tablet use a chemist or doctor in their communication. Why? Because they are using an expert in their field to build trust and credibility into their communication activities and brand – they are using an opinion former. *Opinion leaders* are people who through reasons such as their social standing or closeness to us, or general credibility, we listen to.

The product adoption process (see Chapter 5) is a useful model to illustrate how consumers can be influenced by others. In the marketplace, there are many different types of people who adopt new products at different speeds and junctures. The different types of adopters are not even spread through society:

- innovators represent about 3 per cent of the population;
- early adopters 12 per cent;
- early and late adopters tend to represent the majority of the population;
- laggards represent the final 12 per cent of the population.

The model can also be used when planning a communication strategy.

Example: During first tutorials with new UK students, lecturers go through the module handbook with them and explain the subject and mode of study. They explain the syllabus, the assessment, the reading list and which books are recommended. Before entering the classroom most students don't know the books on the reading list; however, if one book (from a list) is recommended, the students are more likely to purchase the recommended one. The publishers don't directly target individual students when raising awareness of their existence and trying to sell them. What academic publishers do is target the lecturers. Why would a publisher spend thousands of pounds trying to target 1.2 million UK students when they can target a few lecturers, who in turn will target the masses? The teaching staff to help to diffuse publishers' books to the intended market, saving time, money and stress.

The underlying concept here of using innovators, early adopters, opinion leaders and opinion formers is a key one that is used throughout the communication industry. Next time you see adverts or sales promotional activity, stop and think. Are they using any opinion leaders or formers, innovators, or early adopters to diffuse the message and product through the market?

As mentioned in Chapter 5, PLCs are getting shorter and there's a need to hit the ground running when launching new products so as to penetrate the market as quickly as possible. Time is short to recoup all development costs, break even and start to make a profit. Use a two-staged communication process and find and target the innovators and early adopters, who in turn can help you quickly spread your message and offering throughout the market. The use of opinion formers and opinion leaders can also help you establish trust and credibility more quickly.

From the last couple of examples you can see that one of the key reasons for using marketing communication is to support customers as they make purchase decisions. Whether raising awareness of new products we are about to launch, promoting a unique feature or offering money off your next purchase, marketing communication is inextricably linked to this process.

There is a variety of marketing communication techniques and tools that can be used to achieve a large number of differing objectives. The skill here is in understanding which tool, or combination of tools, to select to achieve a given set of objectives. This will be the focus of the following section of this chapter.

How to communicate a message

At this point we need to look more closely at the different techniques that can be used to send messages. The range of tools is known simply as the 'communication mix'. Some use the term 'promotional mix' but this can be confusing as it could be taken to refer to 'sales promotion' rather than 'communication' – if you keep terms clean and simple, the less confusion there will be.

Before deciding which communication tools to use to transport your message from sender to receiver, there are a number of factors to consider that will help you choose the most appropriate communication tools, and indeed, the configuration of the message you send.

What do we need to take into consideration when choosing our communication tools?

There are a number of important factors to consider, as follows.

Target audience/receiver

Who are they? Try to be as detailed as you possibly can. Do you have research based upon their lifestyle choices? Reading habits? What TV programmes they prefer to view? Hobbies they engage in? The deeper understanding you have of your receiver, the richer and more focused your encoding and the actual message you create.

Message and objectives

What do you want to say? What are the objectives of your message? Are you trying to raise awareness? Convey key benefits of your product, brand or service? Stimulate a two-way communication process? Increase your sales and market share? If you have focused objectives, it will be easier to develop the message you wish to convey.

Brand

What does it stand for? What are the personality and values of the brand? Do you want to convey them in the communication?

Budget/costs

How much are you going to spend? This is a key determinant of your communication choices. Indeed, whether strictly correct or not, the budget you have will largely determine the choices of communication tools available to you.

Competition

How good are their communications? As a matter of course and practice, you should always be monitoring your competitive environment (see Chapter 2). What communication tools do they use? How often? Are they successful? Are you centring your communication and message on a product or service? If so, what points do you need to exemplify?

After considering the above factors, you also need to think about the customers in more detail and then select the most appropriate strategy to reach them with your message. These strategies are often referred to as the 'push', 'pull' and 'profile' strategies.

Push strategy

A push strategy is used to 'push' stock down through the marketing channels from one intermediary to the next. In this case, the customer is another business.

Example: A manufacturer may develop a sales promotion encouraging a retailer to increase its monthly order to receive a greater price discount and advertise it with posters via the mail and its sales force.

Pull strategy

A pull strategy is used to entice the end-user to come into stores to ask for and purchase products and services. Here, the customer is the end-user.

Example: A manufacturer may develop a second sales promotion aimed at end-users to entice them to purchase its product by advertising in store and on the pack that if they buy one of the advertised products they will receive a second free (BOGOF – Buy One Get One Free).

Profile strategy

Many organisations may wish to communicate about issues other than their products and services. They may want to communicate with their stakeholders – any person, group or organisation that has a vested interest in the organisation – on issues related to their corporate personality, identity, image, etc. In this case, the customer is any or all stakeholders.

Now we understand more about how the process of how communication works, we can develop our knowledge of the tools we use to communicate to our customers/receivers. These tools are commonly referred to as the 'communication mix' and they include:

■ advertising;
■ sales promotions;
■ public relations (PR);
■ personal selling;
■ direct marketing;
■ sponsorship.

But, communication doesn't end with this list. These tools are the most frequently mentioned, but there are many other communication techniques, often enabled by new technologies; see Figure 8.3.

Many language theorists argue that written words are more powerful than spoken ones. Most marketers (academics and practitioners alike), however, believe that 'word of mouth' is the most powerful means of communication. Table 8.1 highlights the key objectives of each communication tool and their advantages and disadvantages.

Co-ordinated marketing communication (CMC)

When organisations develop communication campaigns, they usually use one or more of the tools from the communication mix to achieve their objectives. This is known as 'co-ordinated marketing communications'. The different communication tools do slightly different jobs (as shown in Table 8.1) and blending a selection of them together in an effective campaign can be beneficial. How? Wider audiences can be reached, a consistent message can be delivered, reducing confused and mixed messages, and there is a greater chance of penetrating the noise and being remembered.

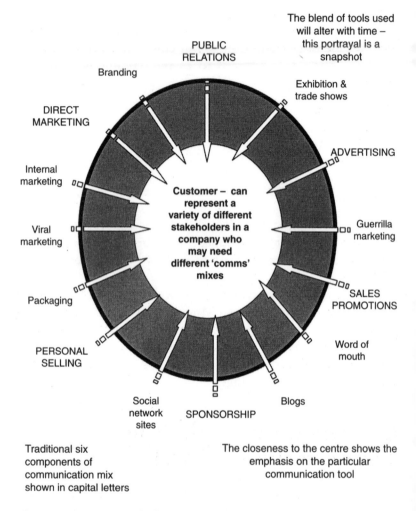

Figure 8.3 *Expanded communications mix*

The use of communications agencies

If you are inexperienced at choosing the most appropriate communication tool(s) to achieve your objectives and if you have the resources available, it would be wise to secure the skill and knowledge of a communications agency.

Table 8.1 *Communication tools compared*

Comms tool	Examples	Advantages	Disadvantages
Advertising	TV advertising Newspaper/ magazine advertising Cinema advertising Banner advertising Can be used effectively in the B2B and B2C markets	Can be cost-effective per person reached Repetition of ads aids memory Long-term image can be created Creativity used in some media choices can cut through noise	Impersonal Indirect Passive – people can zap TV ads, ignore magazine ads, etc Can be expensive particularly in up-front costs Can be difficult to evaluate
Sales promotion	BOGOF Competitions Free prize draws Money-off coupons Loyalty award schemes Bundles Can be used effectively in the B2B and B2C markets	Can add value Can act as an inducement Short-term tactical tool Everyone likes to think they've got something for less	Need to understand the laws and regulations governing this area Credibility – they shouldn't be used too often Give great care to forecasting projected sales
Public relations	Editorial coverage Press conferences Launch themes Open days Media relations Great to use in B2B and B2C markets Good for SMEs and charities	Cost-effective Further credibility compared to advertising and sales promotion Great for developing relationships	Difficult to evaluate Difficult if not impossible to control eg, media
Personal selling	Sales assistants in retail Sales representatives Key account managers (KAM) Use of KAM in B2B market is crucial Use in B2C market is extremely effective	Personal Direct Good to get feedback from customer. Timely feedback Use to form relationships, particularly in B2B market.	Expensive Suffers from 'people' problems' Investment in training and customer service skills required

Table 8.1 *continued*

Direct marketing	Direct Mail Direct Response advertising Telemarketing Effective tool to use in B2B and B2C market	Personal Direct Easy to evaluate in comparison with other tools. Two way communication process	Can lack credibility due to association with junk mail. Extreme care required with security of personal data. Keep up to date with the Data Protection Act.
Sponsorship	Programmes Events Sports teams Personalities	Raises brand awareness and corporate image Can portray positive associations between sponsored and sponsor	Difficult to evaluate What happens if what you have sponsored receives negative press?

There are basically two types of agency you can choose. There are the huge full service agencies such as Saatchi and Saatchi that can create, develop, plan and execute any manner of communication campaign as they employ specialists in all aspects of communication and have vast resources. Alternatively, if you are convinced that you wish to, say, only use PR, then you can engage the services of an independent specialist PR agency. This would be generally cheaper as they don't have high overheads to recoup. Whilst they could create fantastic PR for you, additional types of communication, such as a sales promotion, may be required. You would then have to secure a second agency to plan and execute your sales promotional activity for you and you would have to cross co-ordinate the campaigns yourself. The benefit of using a full service agency is that it houses all communication specialists under one roof and can therefore co-ordinate all communication activities on your behalf – however, it comes at a cost.

Key points

- Communication is a process. It isn't linear.
- All key communication messages should be encoded so that the target receiver can decode and interpret the message successfully.
- A feedback mechanism must be integrated into any campaign whether it is a simple sales promotion or sophisticated advertising campaign.
- Noise is a cause for concern. This variable needs to be taken into account when developing and implementing any communication campaign.
- A two-stage communication process is always useful. The use of innovators or opinion leaders and formers helps to diffuse the message quickly to the intended receiver.
- Communication activities are often used to make customers aware of our products, services, brands and activities. We also need to keep them informed of any changes or news.
- There are three basic strategies that can be used in communications: push, pull or profile strategies.
- The communication mix consists of all the communication tools available to a marketer. The key ones are advertising, sales promotion, public relations, personal selling, direct marketing and sponsorship. Each has its own role, advantages and disadvantages.

Activities

Use Google to navigate to any well-known brand or organisation's website. Many use their website to house their current or more recent press releases and they also often contain a copy of their latest sales promotional campaigns and advertisements.

Next time you are reading a newspaper make a mental note of any advert that catches your eye. What is it that has made you notice it compared to the others? Try to identify who you believe the target market to be. How have the message and creativity been encoded?

Next time you are watching TV identify if any opinion leaders or opinion formers have been used in the adverts. Who has been chosen and why?

If you're sat on a train or in a traffic jam on your way to work, have a look around you. Can you see any posters? Billboards? If you do, again, who do you consider the target market to be? How has the message been encoded? Are any opinion leaders or formers being used?

Create a grid on a piece of paper and write down the key tools in the communication mix on the left-hand side of the paper. Across the top, write the headings: examples, objectives, advantages and disadvantages. Try to fill in the grid and test your knowledge of the role of each of the key communication tools. They each do a slightly different job and fulfil a different role, and you need to absorb this information before all else.

Questions

1. What does the term 'decoding' mean?
2. Why is communication a process and not linear?
3. What is the difference between an opinion leader and an opinion former?
4. If you need to provide an incentive or be particularly persuasive to increase your sales on a particular product line, what communication tool would be the most appropriate to use?
5. Identify the objectives that advertising can achieve.
6. Why is PR often referred to as a 'softer' communication tool than say advertising?
7. Personal selling can also be a persuasive tool to use. Why?

Services marketing vs marketing services

One of the major world trends in recent years has been the dramatic growth in services; 85 per cent of UK GDP comes from services (ONS, 2007; see www.ons.gov.uk). The growth of services is due to rising affluence, more leisure time and the growing complexity of products that require servicing.

What is 'services marketing'?

This question may seem pedantic, but it is the key to better understanding the increasingly important area of services. To answer this let's first identify some:

- hairdressing;
- travelling on a plane;
- renting a hotel room;
- banking;
- advice from a lawyer.

These are examples of services as the core service is intangible. There's nothing physical to grasp, say, when attending the bank. The bank doesn't manufacture a product in the traditional sense. It just provides a service – it facilitates but it doesn't make things.

Now consider companies that sell warranties that potentially could last years. The core product (refer to Chapter 5) is a tangible thing whereas the warranty is an intangible service that is sold (often lucratively) to the client. This is marketing a service.

Example: The Apple iPhone was launched in the UK exclusively through O2. The phone had a list price of around £240 and was not available on a pay-as-you-go basis. Customers had to enter into contracts of 18 months at up to £35 per month. O2 is not the manufacturer and was simply marketing a service – a service that featured a successful launch with huge demand fed by an effective 'pull' promotional campaign. Some observers criticised the overall cost of the phone plus contract, but you have to ask yourself, what would it take for you to queue overnight to buy a product or service? It's hard to criticise customers who are so motivated to buy new products – it's so rare.

What makes up a service?

First of all not all services have the same degree of customer involvement. A visit to a bank's ATM (cash machine) is a low involvement encounter whereas taking part in a body massage involves a high degree of involvement. The degree of involvement impacts on the level of customer expectations. This doesn't mean that customers are happy if the ATM is empty! Most commentators agree that the key components that make up a service are intangibility, inseparability, perishability, variability and ownership. Let's look at them in more detail.

Intangibility

Services cannot be seen, tasted, felt, heard or smelled before they are bought, eg people undergoing cosmetic surgery cannot see the result before the purchase.

Inseparability

Services cannot be stored and sold later, or separated from the providers, whether the providers are people (lecturers, hairdressers or doctors) or machines such as cash dispensers.

Perishability

Services cannot be stored for later sale or use, such as flights. Even if an airline has not sold all the seats on a particular flight, the plane is still going to take off, creating a lost revenue opportunity on the empty seats. Some doctors have started charging for missed appointments (with 250 million GP appointments in the UK each year, even 1 per cent missed visits can have a dramatic effect). Missed appointments are missed opportunities, some of them revenue-earning – the time has perished and cannot be re-captured. So a key challenge for service providers is better demand management. In practice, the nature of a service is that 'manufacture' and consumption are simultaneous.

Variability (sometimes referred to as 'heterogeneity')

The quality of the service is dependent on the person or organisation providing it and so it will vary. This extends beyond who delivers services to include when, where and how they are provided. In restaurants, how much do you pay for the food, the service or the ambience?

If your company suffers from unacceptable levels of variability the solution lies with either standardisation or training, or a combination of both.

Ownership (or more accurately non-ownership)

Unlike products, customers do not secure ownership of services. Rather, they pay to secure access to the service. Car rental companies allow full use of the car but the ownership of the car remains with them. New technologies increasingly blur the line. For example, in music downloading the consumer doesn't own the music; rather he or she owns the right to play the music under certain conditions. As to who owns the 1s and

0s on the consumer's computer ... we'll leave that for others to ponder! Bill Gates argues that it's only a matter of time before TV studios start streaming shows around the world. TV schedules could become a thing of the past sooner than you might think. Look at the enormous amount of content streamed by the BBC, which is one of the world's largest providers of such services.

Example: With broadband speeds ramping up, download services are going to increase. Virgin already offers a wide range of interactive (or on demand) films, music and TV shows. It is moving inexorably towards offering a platform where voice, data, TV and mobile (known in the trade as quad play) interact seamlessly.

The extended marketing mix for services

At this point you need to consider the practicalities of services marketing. You need to amend your marketing mix as the traditional 4Ps (see Chapters 5 to 8) aren't sufficient – hence the introduction of the 'extended marketing mix for services'. This develops the traditional 4Ps by adding three new elements: people, process and physical evidence to form the 7Ps.

People

Simply put, people are your key assets. It is people who provide the service, and their manner, tone, knowledge, ability, body language and appearance can have a profound effect on the customer experience and the overall quality of the service.

Training is always essential and you must pay particular attention to recruitment as training motivated staff is always easier. Armstrong (2006) suggests that employees need to be motivated to change their behaviour and that it is wrong to assume that one approach to motivation fits all. Wise words!

Process

For retailers, service tills (EPOS) and Radio Frequency ID tags (RFID) are visible elements of process systems, whereas booking systems for hotels or concert venues represent behind the scenes elements. Process can have a major impact on the quality of service provided and the overall customer experience. Being told, 'Sorry, the system is down' or, 'Sorry, we don't seem to have your booking' does not enhance the customer experience.

Professor Michael Baker, a key figure in UK marketing over the last 30 years, argues against the term 'customer relationship management' (CRM), which combines the management of relationships and the systems and processes required to do this in a fast and efficient way. Instead he offers the term (and approach) of 'customer satisfaction management'. Wholly preferable! Operational aspects and systems are important but not at the expense of customer focus, particularly in a service environment (more on this in Chapter 11).

Physical evidence

(Calling it evidence would be easier all round but then it would be 6Ps and an E, which is less snappy!) The environment is important – internal and external appearance of premises, waiting areas, or equipment. Also, if your service deliverers are customer-facing, then appearance is an issue.

Challenges facing service providers

Having considered the tools, it's appropriate to reflect on challenges facing your company when providing services. First have no doubt that consumers are more discerning and prepared to move if they're not satisfied with the service.

Sometimes problems occur because of the perception of the service rather than the reality. Another complexity is that often services are 'unsought' in that customers may be unaware of the need for some services. Not all consumers can clearly articulate their needs and may become frustrated. Services can't be tested before purchase, hence there's a degree of risk.

As if this weren't enough, hyper-competition means that moving from one provider to another is easy. Competitive advantage can be obtained by delivering consistently higher quality service than your competitors. Learn more about your clients and customers through rigorous marketing research focusing on their expectations and perceptions. Service quality can be measured although it's difficult and you may wish to seek outside help.

At this point it's worth considering that you may be providing services to colleagues in other departments of your company or within the same parent organisation; see Figure 9.1.

Internal marketing is essential if you're to satisfy the end-user. At times you must sell the benefits to your colleagues. Get them to see the big picture if customer service expectations are

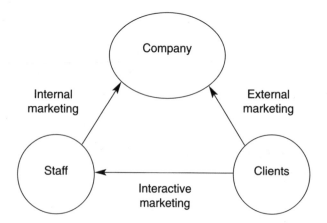

Figure 9.1 *Service profit chain (adapted from Kotler et al, 2005, p. 635)*

to be exceeded and not just met. Many of us carry out internal marketing on a regular basis. Consider the role of IT support; there really is more to it than, 'Have you switched it off then back on yet?' Modern IT departments increasingly talk about satisfying customers. To be effective, services and/or internal marketing needs top management to be fully committed, which sadly isn't always the case.

Marketing charities and small businesses

Kotler recognised long ago that there's more to marketing than Adam Smith's idea of a simple transaction. Kotler's social marketing theory extends to charities that are government funded (occasionally referred to as B2G – business-to-government). Even though the charities don't sell in the traditional fashion they still provide services for which they receive funding. Today charity managers are under increasing pressure to meet stakeholder expectations, so it is appropriate to consider them in more detail.

Charities

That charities exist to create a better society is inarguable, with the vast majority of people considering charities to be trustworthy. Most people use or support charities in some way and the sector makes a substantial contribution to the UK economy, with over 200,000 registered charities generating a turnover of over £32 billion and employing almost 600,000 paid staff.

Example: In 2006 it was estimated that voluntary sector organisations brought £3 billion to the Yorkshire and the Humber regions, but vital services have since been under threat because of changes in European Objective grants and the Single Regeneration Budget. The EU has expanded to 27 member states and new members are attracting more funding.

This confirms the need for charities to monitor the micro and macro environments. Many charities became over-dependent on external funding, which often diminishes their long-term marketing planning. In these days of changing funding, financial security is often no longer guaranteed.

Today businesses are more like charities with CSR and sustainability platforms, whereas charities are more like businesses with professionally run marketing campaigns. It's no longer a case of raising enough funds. Stories exist of larger charities having multi-million pound reserves and yet still heavily promoting themselves and driving fund-raising campaigns. Their argument is that it is too risky to drop out of the public's view. Also, the life cycles of funding, processes and services are constantly reducing and charities face increasing pressures. However, lack of resources and (often) heavy senior management workloads have stifled strategic marketing development.

Marketing generally, and particularly research, is an area of weakness for charities and many acknowledge the need for change. They need to market themselves in a co-ordinated way rather than rely on their usual ad hoc approach. That said, charities have always been willing to adopt a flexible approach to marketing and income generation, with staff often having the freedom to develop activities in effective and efficient ways. To be able to assess a voluntary sector organisation's marketing capability it is necessary to consider its size, as most charities are also small businesses or small-to-medium sized enterprises (SMEs).

The existing marketing audit tools (Chapter 10) were mainly developed for use by larger companies and the circumstances and characteristics of SMEs are different. The Charities Commission stated that 75 per cent of registered charities turn over less than £250,000. Hence they're likely to employ less than 250 staff and predominantly comprise SMEs. This being so, it makes sense to consider the impact of business size on marketing in more detail.

Small businesses

In 2001 SMEs accounted for 99 per cent of UK enterprises; the sector is crucial to the success of the UK economy. Recent estimates suggest the SME sector's annual turnover exceeds £1 trillion. If accurate, this represents nearly half of the UK's private sector economic activity.

What specifically is an SME?

The EC definition (2003/361/EC) states that SMEs should be 'independent' and employ less than 250 people. Further to this, companies that have nine or fewer employees are classed as micro-enterprises.

According to Gilmore *et al* (2001) SMEs have characteristics that dictate their approach to marketing:

■ the inherent characteristics and behaviours of the owner/manager;
■ size limitations and the stage of development;
■ limited resources (such as finance, time and marketing knowledge);
■ lack of specialist expertise (owners tend to be generalists);
■ limited impact in the marketplace.

McDonald argues that marketing planning is an essential activity, but many SME owners deem it unnecessary. They regard marketing as something more relevant to large organisations. This may be due to key marketing texts failing to provide SME managers with practical marketing guidance. If in doubt, SMEs should seek external advice – their local business school will often be able to provide cost-effective assistance.

It's impossible to apply a single rule to all SMEs; they're simply too diverse. Many exhibit entrepreneurial behavioural patterns whilst having little structure, whereas others are long-standing and well established, with structures comparable to larger companies. These differing attributes are shown in Table 9.1.

Table 9.1   *Attributes in relation to company size*

	Weaknesses	Strengths
SMEs	Poor finances Weak market presence	Flexibility Speed of response Independence
Large enterprises	Inertia Politicised Slow response	Strong brand Financial stability Economy of scale Professional management

These SMEs create an interesting paradox as they could be in a 'win-win' scenario, having the strengths of both SMEs and larger companies, or they could be in a 'lose-lose' situation, having only the weaknesses of both, or a combination. Whatever the scenario, it will impact on their approach to marketing. As service providers they need to train their staff to minimise variability, but studies by the Chartered Institute of Personnel Development show that SMEs undertake less formal training than their larger counterparts.

The financial restrictions faced by many SMEs, coupled with the time demands on the owner/manager undoubtedly contribute to the lack of co-ordinated marketing in many SMEs. These barriers should not prevent the adoption of two key marketing tools, namely PR and networking.

PR has many benefits and few downsides for SMEs. There is a wide range of third parties, from agencies to consultants or your local business school. One of them will be able to help at an affordable budget. Another tool that is often used intuitively is networking. Nowadays there are many events suitable for SME managers such as those run by the Chambers of Commerce. Also don't underestimate the potential for networking sites. It's not all Facebook and Gurgle (Mothercare's social network site – great name!). Try Linkedin, which is a business-related network site that's been operating since 2002: www.linkedin.com.

Key points

■ Service industries are growing and are a major driver for economic growth.

■ Service quality can be used to achieve competitive advantage. The drive to improve service quality is a top priority. To do this you must establish clients' requirements and then set internal standards for service delivery.

■ Customers are increasingly willing to move.

■ Analyse internal implications – eg training needs and restructuring, and develop training programmes appropriately.

■ Set up systems to measure and monitor success and review them frequently.

Activities

There are many 'tools' to assist your marketing efforts. It's worth visiting exhibitions where you can see the products and take part in seminars, which tend to practical and helpful. One such in the UK is the Technology for Marketing show. You can see the details at www.t-f-m.co.uk.

How to create a marketing plan

McDonald (2008) gives an excellent account of the tools used in marketing planning to which this chapter will refer (where necessary). If the lack of marketing planning is a serious concern in your company you're strongly advised to read McDonald. In the meantime this chapter will consider the main issues of marketing planning and will seek to offer guidance through what can be a difficult area.

Marketing planning ultimately involves having a longer-term view on how you market your company. In terms of your 'planning horizons' we're talking years not months. Some commentators consider the following to be reasonable guidelines:

- Short term: 1–3 years.
- Medium term: 3–5 years.
- Long term: 5+ years.

Don't simply accept these parameters. Instead. ask yourself whether this rings true in your industry/business. As discussed earlier, PLCs are shrinking and it may be feasible to consider 18 months for your company and its industry. The important thing is to look as far forward as you consider sensible. Since we're talking planning (potentially) years ahead, the thorny issue of strategy arises.

Many books cover strategy and many careers have been forged on the back of the subject. Opinions range widely on its relevance. Practitioners (often correctly) argue that the theories emanate from ivory towers with no basis in reality. Academics counter by saying that without a theoretical foundation there's no basis for measuring the effectiveness of industry choices. The truth is probably somewhere in the middle – isn't it always? However, in simple terms strategy still comes down to: *Where do we want to be and how do we get there?*

Gap analysis

As is often the case the hardest part can be knowing where to start! A common way to address this is to carry out a gap analysis; see Figure 10.1.

A gap analysis can help your company with its strategic development process. Simply put, it illustrates where the company is now and then a forecast is carried out to identify the target point after a set period of time. In larger companies

Figure 10.1 *Gap analysis*

this is often measured in terms of turnover but do this with caution. If your turnover is up 50 per cent in three years you may well be delighted, but if the market has grown 100 per cent in the same timescale you've got a problem. You've lost market share to your competitors and this could have dramatic effects. Growth in profit is often safer but market share is better.

This applies to most companies big and small, profit-making or charity. You may elect to measure your success against some other criteria such as brand awareness or customer satisfaction. These can be measured but some skill is needed and you may want to consider enlisting outside help.

Gaps have to be addressed if your organisation is to achieve its potential. You then have alternatives: to reduce the objectives or to seek to raise performance (ie over-deliver). The latter can be achieved by reviewing the opportunities available to your company. McDonald (2008) argues that gaps can be either operational or strategic.

Operational gaps

These can be filled by a number of methods such as improving organisational productivity, reducing costs or increasing prices. This links to earlier discussions on extending the maturity stage of the PLC where you would seek to stimulate sales or find alternative uses of existing products.

In order to decide where to focus these operational methods, the company's core competencies should be determined. A core competence should significantly contribute to the perceived customer benefits, should be difficult for competitors to imitate and provide potential access to a wide variety of markets. Core competencies are where managers link internal skills with resources such as technology in such a way that employees can react efficiently and effectively. Much valuable work was undertaken in this area by Prahalad and Hamel.

Strategic gaps

These can be addressed by finding new user groups, entering new segments, geographical expansion, new product development and/or diversification. When addressing strategic gaps, it's essential that you honestly assess your company's attitude to risk. Do you speculate to accumulate or would you rather go for organic incremental growth? Neither is automatically better than the other, but if you're risk averse you don't want to plan for huge growth (known as diversification where you aim to sell new products into new markets). High risk, aggressive approaches can take you furthest away from your existing strengths and capabilities, according to McDonald.

Returning to our definition of strategy, assuming we now know where we want to be, the next key decision is on how we get there. Again, acres of library shelf space are dedicated to this thorny question. Ultimately, 'how we get there' can be distilled into the following process:

- mission or vision statement;
- objectives;
- strategy;
- tactics;
- evaluation (many models fail to include a monitoring or feedback loop).

What's the difference between 'mission' and 'vision' statements?

A mission statement should reflect the raison d'être of your company – its purpose. They vary widely from a few lines to comprehensive statements concerning a wide range of factors such as why the company exists, how it operates, and what sort of company it purports to be. Often (most importantly) they define the customers and the benefits offered. Vision statements tend to be somewhat nebulous, offering direction but often without specifics. This book is concerned with providing practical guidance, so mission statements are discussed below.

Mission statements

A mission statement generally expresses your company's overall purpose. Ideally it should be a good fit with the values and expectations of your key stakeholders. A worry for managers is that companies that lack clarity in what they seek to achieve (ie their mission) often have employees who lack direction. Employees need to engage with a progressive, aspirational, grounded vision of the company if they're to be fully motivated to drive through any changes.

The core elements of a mission statement are as follows:

■ raison d'être – essence – purpose;
■ long-term view – strategy;
■ area of company involvement – products or services;
■ core competences – key strengths and benefits to customers;
■ policies – standards – attitudes, eg corporate social responsibility (CSR);
■ value systems, eg fair trade;
■ customers.

The danger in providing a list is that it can be misconstrued as 'one-size-fits-all'. For it to work, you must tailor your mission statement to serve your company's interests and to inform your customers of the value you can add for them. You may consider all or some of the above for your mission statement. However, bear in mind mission statements that aren't customer-centric need to be treated with caution if not contempt.

Influences on mission statements

Mission statements can be inherently political with stakeholders seeking to assert their vested interests. When carrying out consultancy work with large companies it can be enlightening to ask the question 'What should your mission statement be?' Light blue touch paper and retire! Johnson *et al* (2005) argue that the key influences on mission statements are:

■ corporate governance;
■ whom the organisation should serve;
■ accountability and regulatory framework;
■ stakeholders;
■ business ethics;
■ cultural context.

Objectives or strategies – what's the difference?

This is a good question that floors many practitioners (not to mention a fair few academics!). First of all, strategic marketing is not the same as a marketing strategy. Also, an aim is a not a SMART objective. Confused? Let's consider a diagrammatic aide; see Figure 10.2.

Strategies must provide direction whereas objectives (and tactics) are the tools used for implementation. The CIM suggests that a corporate objective is a primary objective of a company expressed in financial terms. At the top level of larger organisations corporate objectives are often set in terms of profit, since this will satisfy (usually remote) shareholders. The vast majority of businesses are small hence this doesn't apply – in the case of SMEs it's usually the owner/manager who needs to be satisfied and this is often shaped by his or her personality or attitudes.

So you've nailed down your mission statement, your staff are motivated and now you have to deliver the goods. Ultimately theory without implementation is a waste of space. You need objectives that are practical.

Objectives

As a general rule it's better if objectives are SMART (as discussed in Chapter 4). Marketing objectives often incorporate two key areas: product development, where you seek to sell existing products to your existing client base; and market development, where you sell existing products to new markets.

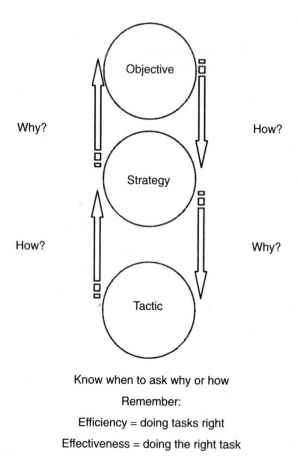

Figure 10.2 *Strategic, objective and tactical flows*

It's worth noting that larger organisations work in strategic business units (SBUs) that often have different markets to address. Think of the Virgin empire and its enormous range from music to trains to planes to credit cards – all have markets that differ in terms of size, type and condition. An effect of this is what may be deemed strategic at the corporate level becomes an objective at the SBU level.

Budget

In a strategic marketing plan there should be a detailed budget for the first year of the plan, according to McDonald (2008). The budget needs to follow the SMART objectives. Indeed, budgets need to be related to what the whole company wants to achieve, which makes the resulting budget more likely to be realistic. The results can be broken down into the different market segments, therefore allowing analysis of how well the marketing mix has worked on specific target sectors. Ideally your company should use the budget to contribute to knowing the return on marketing investment (a variant of ROI – return on investment). It makes sense to know the marketing costs associated with differing strategies.

Strategy

Companies must ensure that strategies are working in practice. A recent study by the Institute of Directors found that 80 per cent (of directors) felt they had the right strategies whereas only 14 per cent thought they were implementing them properly.

McDonald suggests marketing strategy is the means of achieving specific objectives and determining how these objectives will be met. The key focuses of the marketing objectives, and therefore ensuing strategy, are products and markets: strategy is the selection of the markets to target, and the services it offers to its chosen markets. To determine the strategic position of your company you can devise a directional policy matrix (DPM); see Figure 10.3.

A DPM is a tool for determining a product's position in your company's portfolio. It can help you to decide which products need greater (or less) focus. However, it has limitations: the circle sizes may not reflect the true situation as the visuals are quite simplistic and positions are often chosen using subjective elements. That said, it can help to simplify things by providing a perspective and is still worth considering.

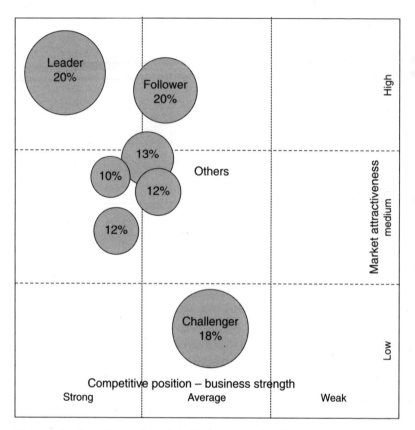

Figure 10.3 *Directional policy matrix (DPM)*

Porter's work has influenced much of the debate on strategy. He proposed three strategic choices: cost leadership, focus or differentiation. This has since evolved to being a straight choice between cost leadership and differentiation. What does this mean to you? To survive and/or prosper your company needs to be perceived by the customer as offering something different. Alternatively, the customer should regard you as offering good value for money. 'Good value' is used rather than 'cheapest', which simply isn't the case. Consumers in general rarely buy the cheapest product available. They do, however, constantly strive to find the best value for money.

Tactics

It's wise at this juncture to consider planning practicalities. Before you can implement your strategies you need to assess the foundations that will provide a springboard for your decisions. This can be done with a 'marketing audit'.

A marketing audit allows you to review internal and external changes that impact on your company. Let's state immediately that all audits are inherently political. They can suffer from clashes with power bases within organisations. You may have to inform a colleague (with substantial experience) that the functions they carry out are not benefiting the customer. This is best done through healthy dialogue that explains the big picture. Those carrying out the audit may be exposed to hostility – it's a case of don't shoot the messenger. Ultimately the message has to be conveyed that it's customers that count.

Earlier we discussed the macro and micro environments and now we'll identify some of the tools. For more detail (in an easily digestible format) see McDonald's book. To consider the micro environment you must reflect on the internal strengths and weaknesses that have affected your company. This covers people and organisations in your immediate sphere of influence. The macro environment refers to the potential (ie future) threats and opportunities that derive from uncontrollable external factors.

Here are some of the tools commonly used to carry out the marketing audit.

Internal audit (micro environment)

Balanced Score Card.
Boston Control Group (BCG) Matrix.
Core Competences Model.
Stakeholder Analysis (customers, competitors, suppliers, distributors, public).
Porter's Five Forces.
5Ms (Money, Men (sic), Machines, Materials, Markets; some people include Minutes – but that would make it 6Ms).
Value Chain Analysis (VCA).

External audit (macro environment)

PEST analysis in all its forms is the tool here: STEEL PIES covers all of the bases and includes sustainability.

Don't be fooled by the array of micro tools compared to the simple PEST analysis. The external analysis is vital and must be carried out diligently. Also, all tools have strengths and weaknesses and you must choose the ones best suited to your organisation and market. If your company is a micro-employer then you're unlikely to have inbound and outbound logistics, so VCA won't fit.

Once you've completed your audit(s) you'll have a wealth of data that will need interpreting. A key tool for this is the SWOT analysis (see Figure 10.4). It is fundamental to a marketing audit as it allows analysis of how you can use strengths to exploit future opportunities or indeed defend threats. It also highlights weaknesses that may be subject to competitive attack in the future. A SWOT analysis portrays the micro analysis in the form of strengths and weaknesses (SWs) versus opportunities and threats (OTs).

SWs are a snapshot of your organisation over recent years and up to the current time. SWs are inward focused, historical

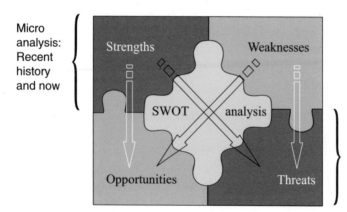

Figure 10.4 *SWOT analysis showing how elements are interlinked*

and seek to identify meaningful information that will enable you to exploit your competencies. OTs are external and future-based. Your reading of the macro environment provides your perception of the issues that will impact on your company over your planning horizon. Having carried out a SWOT you will be in a better position to make improvements; for example you may need to make better use of resources or the skills base of your company could need improving.

Evaluation

There must be a period of measurement and review of any marketing plan. Throughout the ensuing implementation there should be scheduled opportunities to reflect on the plan's effectiveness. All stakeholders should be aware of the time-scales and the need for feedback. You may need to act on these reflections.

If it's so important, why does planning fail?

This is a hugely important question that arises again and again when teaching marketing planning to practitioners. First let's be clear it's not the size that matters. Many studies have noted the positive link between having a marketing plan and business performance in SMEs. Also, many large, well-resourced organizations fail to plan or fail to implement well as a result of their planning. Certainly organisational culture (rather than size) has a lot to do with successful planning.

One of the key causes of corporate failure is plain old 'bad management' and this also applies to marketing planning. This malaise can take the form of weak direction from senior management. If the forecast is simplistic and the resulting target unachievable this will cause problems. Too often the sales target is a wish list: 'It's where we need to be.'

Key points

■ Too little detail will lead to a lack of action whereas too much could lead to 'analysis paralysis'.

■ A lack of skills and resources are key factors that lead not only to poor marketing planning but also to ineffective implementation.

■ It's not enough to carry out a marketing audit and then simply sit on the results saying 'that's that done for another year'. If it has simply become a ritual, an onerous task, then it's unlikely to have the required impact.

■ Being efficient means doing things right, whereas being effective means doing the right things.

Sustainable marketing in the 21st century

The notion of companies being motivated by more than economic profit is not new. Kotler first proposed the notion of 'social marketing' in the 1960s and 'societal marketing' in the 1970s. These relate to social ideas and generally a more ethical approach to marketing. Despite 35 years of research and debate on the efficacy of societal marketing, many practitioners and academics are increasingly concerned that social, ethical and environmental issues have not been fully adopted.

In 1997 Hart coined the phrase 'sustainable development' followed quickly by Elkington's 'triple-bottom-line' (TBL). In TBL the traditional economic focus was replaced with the new foci of social, environmental and economic responsibility. The Hart and Elkington texts are considered to be two of the most important recent contributions on the subject of business and sustainable development.

Since the advent of TBL, the sustainable business development concept has grown, often being referred to as 'people-profit-planet'. This may be new to many practitioners (and academics!) but elements therein have been practised for centuries. Most marketing texts agree that customer attraction, retention and satisfaction are essential for success. This chapter aims to introduce you to the benefits of sustainable marketing, often drawing on sustainable business development theories (see Figure 11.1) using retail as a means of applying the theory.

Why retail? Well, with £250 billion (UK) turnover it's a key economic driver and unlike other service providers, it's based almost entirely upon consumer contact. Other laudable service providers that may carry out sustainable business practices, say those in the FTSE4Good Index, are unlikely to have the complexity of modern major retailers. Also retail is recognised as a fast-changing environment.

Historical perspective

The UK Co-operative movement (affectionately known as the

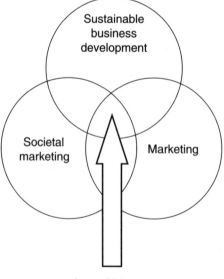

Area of interest

Figure 11.1 *Area of overlap between disciplines*

Co-op) can trace its principles and practices back to the Rochdale Pioneers in the 1840s. Amongst its guiding principles were education, training, information and concern for the community. Often it has been a leader in areas such as product labelling, health education, fair trade and changing the attitudes of local workers towards taking responsibility for their own welfare.

Mainstream retailers have recently followed the Co-op's lead by espousing its green credentials. This has coincided with the rise of consumerism and environmentalism. Environmentalism is poorly represented in the key marketing texts despite becoming increasingly important. That said, consumers are aware of 'greenwashing', so merely stating your green credentials may no longer be sufficient.

When considering the challenges facing your company a key question is 'Why would clients buy our products rather than our competitor's?' Answers to such questions can be crucial. One answer is that consumption is social in that 'buying' is always guided by consumers' thoughts, feelings and actions, which are in turn subject to a range of socio-cultural factors. We take on attitudes, beliefs, opinions and values of others and marketers who are not aware of changes in society run the risk of alienating customers. This is the case with sustainability which, despite being missing from most marketing texts, is increasingly important to key stakeholders.

You say social, I say societal

We live in fast changing times and it's not surprising that a variety of terms are used to represent new, emerging theories. Kotler argues that social marketing relates to the design, implementation and control of programmes seeking to increase the acceptability of a social idea, cause or practice among a target group. This is somewhat limited from a sustainability perspective where global solutions are needed. Also it can be inferred that what matters is the (short-term?) selling of products to the target group. Ironically, sales orientation is now considered a contributory factor in consumers' awareness of greenwashing.

Societal marketing extends Kotler's previous model to include community and consumer dimensions, but it stops some way short of the TBL concept. It offers no specifics with respect to ethics or environmental sustainability but it does introduce the notion of long-term relationships.

None of the key marketing texts offers an adequate definition of sustainable marketing so we'll suggest the following:

> Sustainable marketing (SM) involves principled marketing predicated on the tenets of the triple bottom line. Hence marketing decisions should be ethical and guided by sustainable business practices that ultimately are the only way to resolve the tensions between consumers' wants and long-term interests, companies' requirements, society's long-run interests and the need for environmental balance.

Having defined SM we'll now consider the complex, interdisciplinary nature of the marketing macro environment using profit-people-planet as a template.

Profit

As previously discussed, the importance of scanning the macro environment cannot be overstated. Marketers following the traditional business model of bottom line profit may find themselves reacting to emergent factors that ultimately lead to strategic drift.

Figure 11.2 illustrates how your strategic intentions can be deflected by the adoption or reaction to emergent elements of TBL and/or macro environmental changes and/or changes in consumer values such as the growth in ethical or green goods. Ignoring the macro environment can have a real impact on your profitability.

Example: 'Brownfield' developments have found increasing favour among planners, but retailers seeking development opportunities have complained about a lack of co-operation by

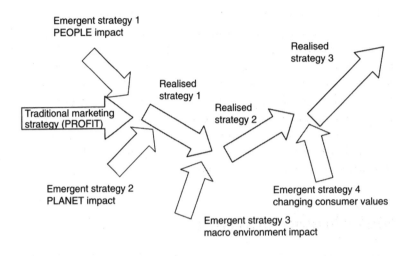

Figure 11.2 *Traditional marketing strategy being deflected by emergent TBL factors*

local authorities, citing severe delays in winning planning approval. This macro environmental interface is interdisciplinary in nature (being between the domains of retail marketing and the built environment) and is typical of others ultimately being driven by governmental environmental policies.

People

A key foundation of TBL is 'people' and there are hundreds of studies that demonstrate the benefits of treating your people well. Many companies claim that their people are their most important 'asset', which begs the question, do they treat their staff as such? A major driver for this chapter is the lack of references to TBL elements within key marketing texts, many of which are recent (being published since 2005) and yet few refer to Elkington and Hart's work. All of the key marketing texts do however refer to (elements of) corporate social responsibility (CSR).

Some organisations recognise the importance of CSR with elements in their mission statements that may include 'green' issues, ethical supply policies and charitable links. A recent development has seen studies discussing CSI or Corporate Social Irresponsibility where the principle of CSR is abused by organisations seeking competitive advantage. Many companies have their reputations tarnished with supply-side scandals with emotive issues such as child labour or 'sweatshops'. Hence with so much of business success depending on supply issues it's important to consider the networks your company employs.

Stakeholder networks

It comes down to this – to what extent can you trust the stakeholders in your network (a term preferred to 'supply chain') to act in ways you deem to be ethically or environmentally sound? There must be differences in terms of differing stakeholders' commitment and you need to manage the relationships carefully. Retailers, for example, are undoubtedly networking organisations and inter-dependent stakeholders therein will need to develop trust in their partners.

Trust and voluntarism

Trust can be shaped by previous experiences and co-operative efforts and on the more general reputation a firm has built up. Socially responsible marketers may also engender trust in consumers and that trust can be grown, say, through positive word-of-mouth. It's logical to recognise the case for measuring and developing trust within your network across a range of issues.

However, patterns exist in the adoption of CSR across differing organisations. Companies that are highly motivated may adopt an idealistic stance or even one of enlightened self-interest, whereas stakeholders on whom they rely may only adopt CSR practices when coerced. This potentially poses a risk for some companies, for example Nike's poor PR following allegations of child labour generated negative publicity.

Community

Larger organisations often engage with the community only reluctantly. When looking to expand, this attitude reduces the site of a new development to 'a plot' and something apart from the community in which it is located. More progressive companies seek to establish relationships in 'place' with local firms, consumers and regulators.

Example 1: Tesco's expansion into the United States, with its Fresh & Easy chain, has been based on successfully engaging the host communities, often adopting a 'softly softly' approach that has contributed to its success. It describes the new chain as 'American stores for American people'. Even its UK tag line, 'Every little helps' is socially inclusive. Undoubtedly Tesco's success is underpinned by long-term research into the needs, wants and desires of its customers.

Example 2: In a £750 million development in Leeds, the developers Hammersons formed a partnership with Leeds City Council. The development (due to open in 2012) is not only one of the greenest ones in UK history but also considers the views of key stakeholders such as community representatives. Hence Hammersons' development will reflect a degree of 'locality' that will benefit the community by avoiding the homogenisation of Leeds' shopping area.

Social inclusion

The last example neatly brings us to the issue of social inclusion, which refers to diverse groups such as those with disabilities, the elderly, those on low incomes and homeless people. Rather than simply complying with, say, disability law, marketers need to be more inclusive and sensitive to stakeholders' needs. Your company may easily benefit from improved PR with the local community, not to mention enhancing your chances of success by favourably influencing the opinions of, say, planners who receive favourable feedback from the local community.

Consumers

By now you will appreciate that consumers often value goods (or services) that appeal both socially and psychological. You probably understand the need to move away from single trans-actions and towards effective management of long-term customer relationships. The issues raised by TBL are often highly charged with emotion as well as clear thinking. Consu-mers attach varying degrees of symbolism and values to their purchases. Increasing numbers of consumers buy food products that are identified as Fairtrade, or other ethically produced goods. The risks are two-fold: if your ethical or environmental profiles fail to align with consumers' values then increased customer losses are likely.

Managing change

Many managers have let operational effectiveness supplant strategy, particularly in cases where constant improvement is often seen as the route to superior profitability. Naturally oper-ations have to keep pace with customer change and the move to sustainable marketing could be one such change. What is needed is not change for its own sake but the right change, and many examples exist of companies that have benefited by moving towards adopting TBL.

A challenge for managers of 'non-enlightened' companies would be to operationalise the move towards sustainable marketing as few models or theoretical constructs exist. It can be argued that too many companies are process- or systems-driven when they should be customer-driven. Think about the term 'customer relationship management' (CRM). Surely this is a misnomer and we all should be seeking 'customer satisfaction management'.

Planet

Environment (aka, it's not easy being green!)

It's no wonder we're increasingly sceptical of environmental claims, hence the rise of awareness of greenwashing. The term 'environment' is used in myriad ways between differing texts and in some cases by the same author. It's prudent to consider such concerns since consumers often readily connect with broader environmental issues. Their environmental interaction is extremely important, featuring intense emotional commitments and involvement that can affect their purchasing decisions.

'Task environment' versus 'servicescape'

In retailing, the 'task environment' refers to the business environments in which retailers function. It's comprised of specific store attributes that consumers use to shape their decisions, eg where to shop. These attributes can be store characteristics (such as cleanliness, spaciousness or layout) or more abstract concepts such as staff friendliness. The task environment is a flawed concept as often consumers deal in general perceptions rather than details. Also, more important, its emphasis is internal and inwardly focused. Marketers who obsess about such metrics may easily miss key customer-centric factors, for example emotive issues such as ethical trading, sourcing local goods, food safety and animal welfare, stakeholder ethics or green concerns. These factors could easily shape buying decisions and yet companies may be distracted by issues such as 'foot-fall' or terminal stock.

Ultimately there's more to service than being served. Indeed the production, delivery and consumption of services revolves around the interpersonal interaction between service providers and consumers. This goes a long way towards establishing customer satisfaction. Every transaction represents an opportunity to show your company in a positive (or negative) light. Understanding customers' needs and having the customer's best interest at heart sends a powerful signal. That said, not all service aspects are equal, hence emotive elements such as ethical goods may have higher consumer value.

Marketers who work in the 'servicescape' are concerned with the relationships they have with consumers. Having a consumer focus raises the servicescape above the task environment, which is a purely operational function. After all, customers make judgements as to whether they belong or feel welcome and when marketers do not understand their perceived discriminations, problems will ensue. Figure 11.3 suggests a template for stakeholders wishing to adopt sustainable marketing (SM). The factors portrayed can impact on multiple TBL elements, for example adopting a CSR policy as part of SM could impact on people and profit.

There has been a sea-change in consumer opinion regarding TBL and it's likely that marketing academics are trailing consumers, progressive organisations and other disciplines. Kotler now argues that marketers' lives will become more complicated. Meeting 'planet' costs may necessitate raising prices. This doesn't automatically mean that the product will be harder to sell, but you'll need to sell the benefits and add value. Also, you'll need to consider where your company should be on the 'sustainability continuum'; see Figure 11.4.

You may choose to commit to a greater or lesser extent. One thing's for certain: in terms of sustainability there's no turning back.

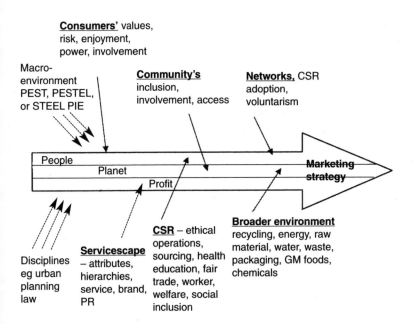

Figure 11.3 *A framework for sustainable marketing*

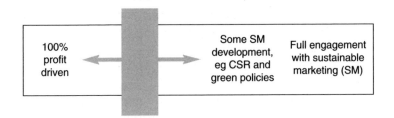

Figure 11.4 *Sustainability continuum*

Questions answered

This chapter provides answers to chapter-related questions and suggestions of further reading materials to add breadth and depth.

Chapter 1. Marketing: separating fact from fiction

1. The marketing concept identifies the customer as being at the heart of all business decisions and central to the entire culture of the organization, thus creating a responsibility for everybody who works with and for the organisation to consider and embrace the importance of the customer on a daily basis.

2. A marketing-oriented organization can hope to see an increase in sales, turnover, profitability, market share and customer loyalty, and an enhanced reputation and competitive edge. Basically, if you satisfy customers, they will come back for more and spread the word.

3. In the long term the initial razzle dazzle of the product will fade, thus leaving a potential situation of falling sales, market share and profitability, and a loss of customer confidence and reputation. These organizations tend in the main to be inwardly focused, thus often missing new opportuni-

ties and threats lurking in the marketplace and marketing environment.

4. Everybody who works with and for an organization is responsible to some degree for its marketing. This is because we all contribute towards creating the customer experience and thus affect their levels of satisfaction.

5. This is a long-term commitment. Strong leadership is required from the top. Continuous training must be given to all current and new staff and the role and importance of the customer must be emphasized in their role. All systems should be considered from a consumer perspective, not just an organisational one. The structure of the organization should be considered – the flatter the better, creating a situation that keeps top management close to the shop floor and hence, the customer and marketplace.

Have a look at the CIM's marketing glossary (see link; accessed Jan 2008). It offers well thought out, succinct definitions: www.cim.co.uk/KnowledgeHub/MarketingGlossary/Glossary Home.aspx.

Chapter 2. The marketing environment

1. The PEST factors constitute the key forces in the macro environment: political, economic, social-cultural and technological.

2. PEST, PESTLE, STEEPLE, EPISTLE, STEEL PIES.

3. The micro environment consists of: customers, competitors, suppliers, distributors and publics.

4. The micro environment is partly controllable and influenced due to the relationships that the organisation has with the relevant parties.

5. The monitoring of the environment is very much dependent upon the nature of the industry, market and environment you see yourself operating in. Ideally, you should be moni-

toring the environment daily, even in a stable climate. The macro environment is turbulent and dynamic – anything can happen!

Always look at the BBC website (www.bbc.co.uk) and the national broadsheet newspapers (eg, www.timesonline.co.uk) to keep an eye on the movements in the environment. Reading magazines/books/articles such as *The Economist* (www.economist.com) is also helpful.

Chapter 3. Customers in all their glory

1. The consumer buying process includes five main stages: problem recognition, information search, information evaluation, purchase decision and post-purchase feedback.
2. If a consumer is making a risky decision whether it be financially risky or personally or socially (or all!), they tend to take their time making the decision, searching for information and weighing up the pros and cons.
3. Factors such as sex, age, occupation, income, personality type, sense of motivation and perception and past experiences will all serve to influence their choices and behaviour.
4. Businesses purchase in significantly larger volumes than consumers; they also have a degree of specialized purchasing skill that the average consumer does not tend to have. The procedures and policies of purchasing by a business also tend to be more formal and often includes several people.
5. Marketers need to understand how consumers and organisations behave when purchasing products and services, not only to influence the process and their behaviour, but also to assist them with additional marketing support. This can help the customer to reduce risk and feel more informed and therefore comfortable when making a purchase decision.

Chapter 4. Using research to make informed decisions

1. Investment in research is crucial to provide accurate data to help make more informed decisions, lower risk and generate greater knowledge.
2. Research can be time-consuming and costly, both financially and through the use of additional resources. A degree of expertise is also required at times.
3. Secondary data is data that already exists in some shape or form. The use of past sales or market research reports, articles and government statistics are all examples.
4. Primary data is data that is collected first hand to help solve the actual research problem and fulfil the research objectives. The creation and use of a questionnaire, in-depth interviews, focus groups, observation and experimentation are all examples of how primary data can be collected.
5. Research objectives serve to provide focus, a sense of purpose and direction to the research. They tend to govern the choice of secondary and primary data and the overall design of the research itself.

Have a look at the following Kogan Page books for further detail: *Market Intelligence* (Martin Callingham, 2004), and *An Introduction to Market and Social Research* (Karen Adams and Ian Brace, 2006).

Also look at a variety of websites: the Market Research Society's Code of Conduct is essential reading for those involved in marketing research. Their website is at www.mrs. org.uk/. Others to peruse are: www.mintel.com, www.datamonitor.com and www.marketing-intelligence.co.uk.

Chapter 5. Product management

1. Classification of products allows the marketer to better understand how customers will purchase the product: how much time they will spend evaluating the purchase, the degree of risk involved and the overall process they will go through when purchasing – and what will influence them. Therefore, this gives valuable information to the marketer to be able to support the purchaser with a variety of associated marketing tools.

2. The intangible component of a product refers to its 'softer' aspects – those that you cannot physically see or touch but which bring significant value to it, eg the brand.

3. The length of PLCs is generally getting shorter. Rapid development and adoption of new technologies, dynamic environmental conditions, strong competition and greater consumer sophistication are some reasons for this.

4. Find new customers/users; find alternative uses for the product; give a facelift to the product to spruce it up and give it a more contemporary feel.

5. You can diffuse products quickly through the use of innovators, early adopters, opinion formers and opinion leaders. These influential people/parties will help influence others to purchase products and services and add credibility.

Look at the large number of products developed by Ford and Coca-Cola. Also have a look at their press sections. The launch of many of their new products are often posted here: www.ford.com and www.coca-cola.com.

The Consumer Electronics Show is probably the largest of its kind in the world and is worth a look (www.cesweb.org).

The research on NPD failures can be found in Armstrong, M and Kotler, P (2007) *Marketing: An introduction*, 8th edn, p 239, Pearson/Prentice Hall, London.

Chapter 6. Right time, right place, right quantity, right condition

1. Increases in the use of technology by consumers, the sophistication of the technology, the greater levels of control, greater potential of immediate feedback and the potential of lower costs, have all contributed to the increase in direct distribution.
2. Intermediaries provide a convenient network of stores, resources and accessibility to consumers. They also provide experience, skills and knowledge of the retail sector.
3. An exclusive distribution strategy would be used to distribute exclusive products. The limited accessibility and availability of such products serves to enhance their appeal.
4. A long channel design allows different intermediaries that all specialise and have knowledge and resources to do their particular job well. It allows further intensive distribution, if sought, and accessibility and often convenience to consumers.
5. Many customers often find that products and services are not available when sought. Many are not delivered on time and when they are, they are often damaged and incorrect in the quantity ordered. All these issues can lead to customer dissatisfaction. Simply put, you may have a fantastic product or service but if you can't get it to market in the right place, at the right time, in the right quantity and in the right condition – your competitors will.

Some websites to consider: www.avon.uk.com and www.easyjet.com are interesting companies to look at as they distribute their products and services through a more direct approach.

Chapter 7. You paid how much?

1. There are so many different variables to take into consideration and to try to balance, which isn't always easy or workable.
2. What price the customer is willing to pay, the nature and price points of the competition, the overall direction and objectives of the organisation and marketing team, the overall cost structure involved and any legal issues.
3. Price is often used to determine a mark of exclusivity and quality and vice versa. Most people associate higher prices with a higher grade of quality.
4. Both – with the marketing team taking the lead. Continuous monitoring of all associated costs is required by the finance team. However, the marketers need to monitor the market, environment, customer and competition at all times to assess any effects on their offering to the market and its price point.

Remember to look at relevant websites. The Office of Fair Trading keeps an eye on a number of companies in terms of their pricing policies and business activities (www.oft.gov.uk).

Chapter 8. How communication works

1. Understanding and interpreting the encoding (signs, symbols) in the message.
2. Because a feedback mechanism is required to filter back into the process. If the communication is going well, we need to know. Alternatively, if it isn't – we also need to know and make adjustments to the campaign and programme if required.
3. An opinion leader is someone who the target market sees as having a social standing and influence generally. An opinion former is such due to their actual expertise, usually through their profession, therefore having credibility.

4. Sales promotion.
5. Raising awareness, informing, educating, persuading.
6. The use of PR is not to increase the bottom line directly, ie to increase sales or profits. Instead it is often used to develop relationships with the organisation's publics, to generate goodwill and trust and to foster relations.
7. It is often face-to-face and so people can be engaged with customers and ask questions and facilitate answers directly in a persuasive yet professional manner if required.

Remember to have a look at websites as well. Here are some to peruse: www.asa.org.uk and www.ofcom.org.uk.

Figure 8.2 is from Fill, C (2006) *Simply Marketing Communications*, p 30, FT/Prentice Hall, London.

Chapter 9. Services marketing vs marketing services

To consider improving your networking check out the business network site, www.linkedin.com.

For recruitment/motivation of employees have a look at Michael Armstrong's book, *Human Resource Management* from Kogan Page, or look at the Chartered Institute of Personnel Development site, www.cipd.co.uk.

For the more academically inclined the following article on SMEs is useful: Gilmore, A, Carson, D and Grant, K (2001) 'SME marketing in practice', *Marketing Intelligence & Planning*, **19**, 1, pp 6–11.

For light reading on SMEs look at: EC (2005) European Commission Recommendation 2005/361/EC http://europa.eu.int/ISPO/ecommerce/sme/definition.html [accessed 25 August 2006].

The figure of the service profit chain is from Kotler, P, Wong, V, Saunders, J and Armstrong, G (2005) *Principles of Marketing*, 4th edn, Pearson/Prentice Hall, London.

Chapter 10. How to create a marketing plan

If you're interested in marketing planning, get hold of Malcolm McDonald's book, *Marketing Planning: Understanding marketing plans and strategy*, from Kogan Page. It hits the nail fairly and squarely on the head. For those teaching marketing planning it's an invaluable resource.

For more on mission statements, see Johnson, G, Scholes, K and Whittington, R (2005) *Exploring Corporate Strategy – Text and Cases* 7th ed, FT Prentice Hall, London. Porter's work on strategy can be found in Porter, M (1980) *Competitive Strategy*, Free Press, New York.

Chapter 11. Sustainable marketing in the 21st century

There's precious little on sustainable marketing even in the key marketing texts. For a range of academic conference papers (which cover a large range of industries around the world) look at: The Corporate Responsibility Research Conference website, http://crrconference.org.

The following book contains a number of informative studies on sustainability including the key Hart and Elkington studies: Starkey, R and Welford, R (2001) *The Earthscan Reader in Business and Sustainable Development*, Earthscan Publishing, London.